THE
LIONESS LEADS
STORIES OF TRIUMPH OVER FEAR

A Collaborative Work Presented by

Dr. Synetheia N. Newby

Purposed Publishing Company, LLC
Bowie, MD

The Lioness Leads: Stories of Triumph Over Fear

ISBN (paperback): 978-1-7370473-3-9
ISBN (e-book): 978-1-7370473-4-6
Library of Congress Control Number: 2021917970

Published by Purposed Publishing Company
www.purposedpublishingcompany.com
Email inquiries to: info@purposedpublishingcompany.com

Printed in the United States of America

Cover designed by Stephen Fortune at Skycon Media, LLC
Editing by Monica Settles
Proofreading by Erica Dyson
Interior design by Matías Baldanza

Contents

THE LIONESS LEADS: STORIES OF TRIUMPH OVER FEAR

I AM COURAGEOUS

I AM UNAPOLOGETIC

MEET THE AUTHORS

CONTENTS

Introduction

BY DR. SYNETHEIA N. NEWBY

THERE'S NO COINCIDENCE that you have this book in your hand. Whether you purchased it as a digital download or as a printed text, or if someone sent it to you as a gift, it's not a surprise. You are holding the stories of fourteen diverse women to experience moments of identification, empathy, understanding, encouragement, inspiration, and motivation. You are also holding this book because the power of the messages on the following pages is what you need in your life right now to overcome your fears. You need this book so that you can live boldly, authentically, courageously, and unapologetically.

You may ask how I know what you need when I may have never met you personally. I know because I am you. I am a woman who has wrestled with fear; sometimes I lost, and other times I won. I am a woman who needs support and the comfort of community with other women. I am a woman who needs encouragement, motivation, and inspiration. I am a woman who gives so much of myself to others, who often feels depleted, and who longs for someone to empathize with my experiences and understand the challenges I face. Like you, I am also a woman who leads others.

I lead as an entrepreneur and as a senior manager in government. You may lead as an administrator, a parent, a faith leader, or a community activist. No matter your leadership role, I know you can identify with the challenges we face as women, in general, and as women who lead. One of the most significant challenges we face is fear. Fear of the future, fear of the unknown, fear of rejection, fear of our power, fear of failing, and even the fear of succeeding. Fear is a part of all our lives, and none of us can escape its visitation. While we can't avoid it, we can determine how we respond and prevail against it. We can choose to be bold, authentic, courageous, and unapologetic when fear says, "shrink, pretend, hide, and make other people feel big while you get smaller." Most of us wear so many hats, and have so many people depending on us, that we rarely find safe places to talk about our fears. Many of us fear being fearful because we see it as a sign of weakness. Let's face it - we can't let people know that under our superhero capes, we are just human beings with real fears. When I think about how we can choose to respond to fear and triumph over it, I am reminded of a beautiful creature: the lioness.

Lionesses are known for their bravery, courage, and assertiveness. They are aggressive, yet nurturing, caring, and protective. Lionesses look after their cubs and train them to look after themselves and to become leaders within their pride. They empower and support their young and are synonymous with what we call a modern woman in business. They are bosses! The thing about a lioness that many people may not know is that they are the backbone of the pride. She is the one who goes out on the hunt and brings the food back for the pride. Strategic in their approach, learning the landscape and terrain, they move slowly at first, stalking their prey, watching their habits and movements. Sometimes they lie in wait for minutes, even hours. Then, they creep up on their prey at just the right time, under the right circumstances, and strike. When the lioness strikes, she moves with lightning speed running at up to thirty-five miles per hour. She is laser-focused on the goal and pursues it relentlessly.

Despite their individual prowess and power, lionesses thrive even more when they are together. I think it's so unique that they are all about sisterhood and community. I believe lionesses realize, just like you and I, that sisterhood and community matter. We are great alone,

INTRODUCTION

but so much more fantastic together. In a community we gain strength, and we learn from one another. In our tribes, we empower and challenge one another to address our fears, and we inspire one another to be our best authentic selves. As women who lead, we are just like the lionesses. We are BACÚ™, meaning we are bold, authentic, courageous, and unapologetic!

Do you see yourself as a lioness?

Do you see how you move strategically, intentionally, and relentlessly?

Do you see your resilience?

I do.

If you can't see it, I think it's because you're not giving yourself enough credit.

The characteristics of the lioness lie within you. You are assertive and courageous even in the face of self-doubt. You have scars from battles you fight and never share. You fall and are counted out but get back up again. That makes you like the lioness. And much like the stories you're about to read from other lionesses like you, you are still growing and evolving into the fullness of the lioness's strength, courage, and bravery. We are triumphing over fear, and so are you. We are a part of the BACÚ™ tribe and are leading in our respective realms of influence. Every day, like the lioness, we are becoming increasingly BACÚ™!

As the reader of this book, you are now a part of the BACÚ™ tribe, too. Welcome to this community of empowering, nurturing, and inspiring leaders. Enjoy the journey with us.

THE
LIONESS LEADS

I AM
BOLD

"The lioness doesn't conform to the habits of the cheetah nor the gazelle. The lioness shows up boldly as the lioness."

Dr. Synetheia

The Lioness Leads Boldly

WE ARE NOT TAUGHT TO BE BOLD. From a young age, we are trained to conform and behave like others. From standing in a straight line in kindergarten to hair norms in the workplace, conformity has been the norm for years. Boldness counters traditionalism and conformity, encouraging vibrancy, showing daring audacity, inspiring confidence and a willingness to take risks. Boldness does not mean fearlessness. Instead, it means feeling, seeing, and acknowledging the presence of fear and deciding to take the risk anyway. Boldness is choosing to risk the displeasure and disapproval of others. It chooses to stand out from the crowd and be the voice of dissent in a room of the majority. Boldness is setting your goals, seeing the potential obstacles, calculating the risks, developing a plan of attack, and pursuing each goal relentlessly and with great audacity. This is what the lioness does in the wild.

The lioness doesn't conform to the habits of the cheetah nor the gazelle. The lioness shows up boldly as the lioness. We become aware of her presence through her visibility, her sound, and her movement—the lioness who is on the prowl moves with confidence. As she relaxes in the grass, watching her cubs, she holds her head high, making her presence and protection known. The lioness does not shrink even as she finds herself surrounded by a gang of hyenas as she hunts for food for the pride. She may feel the fear, but she positions her body, prepared to attack and be attacked. She may win or lose; she may sustain injuries in the fight. Yet one thing remains true: she showed up boldly in pursuit of the goal. If she fails, rest assured she'll still show up again boldly, no matter the fear of being attacked again. And that's the heart of boldness: showing up with audacity, confidence, and without apology when fear says we should not.

Women who lead must be bold like lionesses.
We are the trailblazers.
We are the norm disruptors.
We have audacity.
We will not shrink.

Facing It Head On

BY MARHONDA ECHOLS

I'VE EXPERIENCED BEING FIRST most of my life. I was the first child, the first grandchild to graduate from high school, and the first in my household to both go to and graduate from college. Although being first can be an exciting journey, sometimes it can be really scary, too! There is no blueprint, no note to read, no previous person to call. Although I did fairly well in school, and certainly learned a lot, I was not prepared for the challenges I would face. As a working adult, I received my first disciplinary action.

Throughout my professional career, I've always worked in the Criminal Justice or Human Service field in some capacity. I've worked with victims of crime to help them walk through the criminal justice process and receive resources to help overcome their victimization. I've provided community outreach and education services to partners to help connect my former employer with the community so they would be seen as part of the community and not just another entity that was set on tearing it apart. And in keeping in line with my trend of *"firsts,"* I was hired to lead a brand-new effort focused on helping to improve the outcomes of high-risk youth by connecting them to services and resources that would offer them better opportunities in life. This included not only servicing the clients directly, but also supporting the members in their households.

9

Accepting a position of this caliber was a bold move! While I knew there were components of the job that I could do based on previous work experiences, there were other parts that I simply felt unqualified to handle because I'd never done them before. Although I gave many reasons for why I shouldn't apply, I stepped out on faith and did so anyway. Imagine my surprise when I was not only called back for a second interview, but I was also offered the position! As women, we sometimes allow ourselves to be comfortable in the background or shrink back because we don't feel qualified; but there comes a time when we have to encourage and speak life to ourselves and make the bold move to step out into new territory. Unqualified or not, I was offered the job, and I wasn't going to let anything stop me.

Naturally, building something from the ground up consisted of many moving parts. There were goals and objectives that had to be written, staff that had to be hired and trained, committees that had to be formed to determine how clients would be served, and partners that needed to help provide the identified services. National partnerships had to be cultivated because this was the first initiative of this caliber locally. And of course, there were updates and reports that had to be provided regularly to monitor progress, address challenges, and help justify and secure subsequent funding. I had to lead all these efforts, and I did it with consistent hard work, dedication, support, and determination to successfully launch this initiative.

By year five I had started to find a groove and, for the most part, things were going well. One day it was brought to my attention that one of my part-time staff members may have violated our code of conduct. No one directly involved had come to me, so I decided to make my own note of it and be extra observant by keeping my eyes and ears open. I waited and listened to see if anyone else would say something, but it didn't happen. Another allegation was brought to me that was more serious than the previous one and therefore required immediate action, which was taken. During this same timeframe more trouble occurred.

FACING IT HEAD ON

One of my full-time employees quit abruptly, and I was called into a meeting with my supervisor. I was told that allegations had been made against my character and role as a supervisor. Due to the seriousness of these allegations and the situation with the part-time employee, I was informed that an investigation would be performed by Human Resources and I was to stand by for next steps.

In the blink of an eye, I went from an employee that had only received positive evaluations and commendations to being under investigation. Needless to say, I was devastated. I received this news at the end of the day on a Friday, so I had the weekend to process it. Everything kept replaying in my mind; I hardly slept or ate. I was angry, I was hurt, I was embarrassed, and I had become depressed. I locked myself in my home and I didn't want to see or talk to anyone – including God. That's right, I was so overwhelmed that I couldn't even pray! I was so numb in that moment that all I could do was stare at the walls. I sat in silence, moving from the floor to the bed feeling completely numb. What did I do wrong? What did I miss? Why was this happening to me? What more could I have done that wasn't already done? I debated on submitting my resignation because there was no way I could face anyone after this. In fact, I was sure that I had to quit before they fired me. At least a resignation left me with a little bit of dignity versus a termination!

On Sunday I experienced a breakthrough moment with God. He reminded me that not only was He going to walk with me through this ordeal, but quitting was not an option. Instead of resigning, I made the bold decision to keep showing up. And while showing up meant that I didn't have to pretend that nothing was happening, I couldn't let my circumstances change or consume me. Regardless of who knew of the pending investigation, there was still work that had to be done. After waiting several weeks, my meeting with Human Resources had been scheduled. I had another moment of, *"This is not worth it – just quit,"* but lionesses do not shrink in the face of adversity; we make the bold decision to keep showing up and to keep our heads held high.

Truthfully, as I was speaking with Human Resources, there was a moment in which I wondered if continuing to be honest about my actions was worth it. There were looks of disbelief, rephrasing of questions to see if my answers would change, and shifts in body language. It seemed easier to just say what I thought they wanted to hear, but my boldness required me to stand in my own truth. By the time my meeting concluded with Human Resources, I had learned that instead of me being the first person to be interviewed in an investigation against me, I was one of the last. My entire staff had been interviewed along with others whom I had worked with before.

The investigation with Human Resources resulted in me facing disciplinary action because of how I mishandled the original situation. Instead of hiding and hoping it all went away once it was over, it brought out a strength and fight in me that I didn't know I had. I made the decision to walk with my head held high instead of hanging low because, whether intentional or unintentional, we all make mistakes. Instead of continuing to feel like, *"If someone has an issue with me, it's their responsibility to address it,"* I initiated the hard conversations with my staff. Some conversations included meeting with each of my remaining staff members to learn if I had offended them, to correct it if I had, and to ask what they needed from me to be a better supervisor. This experience caused me to evaluate how I communicate, both verbally and nonverbally, and take responsibility for the good and the bad. I learned to be more mindful of my nonverbal gestures, to ask more probing questions, and be more considerate of my staff's well-being at work. Instead of being angry, I became proactive and learned from my mistakes. My boldness allowed me to become a better version of myself as an individual and as a leader.

In this journey called life, there will be good days and bad days, high points and low points. Not all battles are private and there will be some that are played out publicly. Whatever comes, steady your head and keep showing up. In those moments of adversity that are sure to come, make the bold decision to not shrink back, but to face it head on. Choose to learn from your mistakes and not let them destroy you. Take the time to do the hard work of understanding what went wrong, and committing to make it right. Even in the toughest of times, embrace the lesson that grew you the most, and use that to better equip you for your next challenge.

Reflections

....

....

....

....

....

....

....

....

....

....

....

....

Still Standing

BY STEPHANIE LANE

I STRUGGLED WITH THE FEAR of failure and rejection most of my life. Fear of telling my story. Fear of what others would say and think about it because they couldn't understand what I experienced. Fear of being rejected because of the things that happened to me. Fear of failing in life and not being able to achieve my goals. I was thirty years old when I decided to overcome those fears. This burden was something that I didn't want to hold on to anymore. I was ready to do better for myself, and I made a bold decision to tell my aunt that I was molested at a very young age. The trauma of being molested affected me in so many ways my whole life. After I told my truth, I was able to get the help I needed. That choice to be bold and share my story is how I overcame my fears and started my journey toward healing.

Both of my parents were drug addicts. My mom chose men and drugs over her kids. I knew my dad, but he wasn't in my life very much. As a result, my brother and I would later be raised by my grandparents. I struggled with depression. I was hurt, angry, and confused. I looked for love and found the wrong love in different places. I endured abuse in my relationships and had my first child at sixteen. Because of the trauma and abuse I endured, I became a bitter and promiscuous woman because I felt no one else cared, so why should I? I ran from the hurt that I was feeling instead of dealing with it. I would go to clubs, get drunk and fight. Hurting inside and out and unable to face myself, I turned to the bottle because it was my safe place. I would get so drunk that I couldn't even remember what happened. I had to look at myself and say, *"Stephanie, is this even worth it?"*

I stopped drinking for a couple of months, but my life was still upside down. I would get a job, but I had so much hate in me that I could not perform well. I was mean to everyone and I never got a promotion. I was always written up because my attitude was horrible. I finally had a wonderful supervisor that believed in me and showed me that I didn't have to be unruly or hateful because of the terrible things I've experienced in my life. She helped me, and I worked hard and became her deputy assistant supervisor. My desire was to be a supervisor, but I wasn't ready to become a supervisor as I still couldn't take feedback without getting upset about it. My director sent me to supervisor training and that would later help me to land a position. During this time, I still suffered from depression, so my friends encouraged me to get help for my past trauma, too. Things were going well. I did well as a supervisor and earned raises. I started going to church and I started going to therapy and taking medication. But it only lasted for a little while because my biggest challenges came back into my life - my mother and father.

When my mom came back into my life she was diabetic, strung out on drugs, and in the hospital. I knew it was going to be a struggle. Our relationship was rocky at best since we hadn't faced our past. I went to the hospital and when she regained consciousness, she said that she wanted to die. She didn't die. I took care of her for seven years and during that time was often blamed by her for not caring enough, for stealing her money, and so much more. I was angry at her for not taking care of me and protecting me when I was younger. And even as an adult, she was still causing me pain and hurt. Yet, I was encouraged to pray for and forgive her. I was constantly giving of myself and my time to care for her, often neglecting my own needs. I was working and getting on my feet, and caring for my mother, but I was still depressed.

I still needed care for myself. And only God knew what would come next in my life.

One day I was called from the hospital stating that my dad was on life support and I needed to come quickly. He had legal documents that put me in charge of everything he owned, including his life and care. When he woke up and was able to talk, he grabbed my hand and kept hugging and apologizing to me. He stated that if anything happened to him, all he owned and all decisions about his belongings were to be made by me. I was dealing with not one, but two sick parents that had never been in my life, and both were depending on me because they had burned too many bridges with other people in the family. I cared for them both even though they had never cared for me. I had my kids, my job and staff, and my parents to care for, and I was constantly making sure everyone else was alright, except me. I still had depression. I still needed to heal. I still needed to take care of myself. I had family and friends who prayed for me and encouraged me. I gave myself pep talks, telling myself, *"You're gonna be ok."* But I had to keep putting myself on hold, knowing more was needed to care for myself. I always cared for others despite what I was going through in my own life. But now, I had to make a bold choice to focus on and care for myself.

In July 2020 while I was at work, out of nowhere my chest felt like someone was pulling at it. My phone rang and a woman yelled for me to get to my dad's house because they were performing CPR on him and they couldn't stop until I got there. They had been doing CPR for over twenty-five minutes when I arrived, and there was nothing else they could do. I passed out. I would later find out that he had stopped dialysis two weeks before he died, stating that he was tired and in a lot of pain. I only got six months of time with him out of thirty-nine years of my life, but I think he was trying to get it right with me before he left this world. Enough was enough. I told myself as I prepared for his homegoing, *"I have to be stronger than this."* If I was going to continue in this life, I had to finally put myself first.

Overcoming depression is not something that you deal with once and it is over. I had to choose myself over others in order to get the care that I needed. I had to do things differently if I wanted to stay on the path of healing and health. So, I took action. I first asked for help, but not just for prayer or encouragement. That was good, but I needed more than that. People would tell me, *"You bring the depression on yourself,"* because I had feelings and thoughts about my trauma that would not go away. Those words hurt me, but I continued on my path to healing anyway. I started attending weekly therapy. I took medication to help with my depression. These things are taboo in the African American community, and we often do not talk about their benefits when needed. I felt better as a result of therapy and medication. I no longer felt like I was in a fog, and my mind felt clearer. I could open up more to talk about my past. I also stepped away from people and things that would trigger negative fears and bad habits in my life. I wanted to make sure I did not repeat the same patterns that my parents had, and I told myself that I didn't have to end up like them. I can have a new life; a good life for me and my children.

I have been through a lot in my life, but I have found the courage to stand up and be bold despite my circumstances. I am still doing that to this day while handling life as a mom, caregiver, and supervisor. I make sure to care for myself while I care for others. Sometimes we don't know what our roles in life are going to be, but when it comes, make sure you're ready. You can face anything in life if you have the boldness to love and care for yourself the right way, so that you can be the person and leader you need to be in your life.

Reflections

....

....

....

....

....

....

....

....

....

....

....

....

....

Courage to Speak Up

BY LESLIE BILLUPS

AUGUST 11, 1997 was one of the most devastating days of my life. It was the day that I got an abortion. How could this be? I was only eighteen years old, had just graduated from high school in June, and I had no idea that I was pregnant when I graduated. Upon telling my parents and the father of my child, it was my father's decision to take me to a clinic to *"take care of it."* I had no idea what he was referring to when he said it. As we arrived at the clinic, and I was preparing to fill out the paperwork, it still had not dawned on me that this clinic also specialized in abortions. Once I realized what was happening, my heart dropped and shattered into pieces. As I went back into the room, and the nurse and doctor were speaking to me during the procedure, everything in me became numb. The shock of it all paralyzed me into complete numbness. Shortly afterwards, it was over.

As I left the clinic, all I felt was an emptiness. I was shattered and broken. I went from knowing what was about to happen to now being in shock that it happened. I could not find the words to tell anyone. I was so numb that I could not even cry; I thought something was wrong with my feelings because I couldn't feel. I thought about what just happened. I literally threw my first child away. Who does that? I went from shattered to broken to being angry with myself. All I knew was that I never wanted to experience this feeling again. I never wanted to become pregnant again and I felt ashamed of what I had done. I began to look at myself as someone who could not complete something. I didn't complete my pregnancy by having my child, and this was the moment I began to feel like a failure. I felt like I could not do anything right and I wondered if I would ever be able to do so.

The next seven years of my life took me on a spiritual journey where I confronted my fears of failure, shame, and guilt. This journey led me out of a place of hiding and secrecy to a place of liberty and peace. From 1997-2004 I became pregnant seven times. I had one abortion, three miscarriages, and three live births with my boyfriend, who became my husband. The number seven symbolizes completion and perfection, and I did not understand what God was doing with me during this time, but I learned throughout these years.

After my abortion in 1997 at age eighteen, I became pregnant again in 1998 and miscarried. In September 1999 I gave birth to my first child. For the first full year after having my daughter, I just knew that I was out of the woods. Then suddenly, life took another turn, and I miscarried again in 2001. At this point I felt like giving up on my own life. My body had been through so much and I did not feel like I could endure any more pain and suffering. I had always wanted children, a family, full term pregnancies, and it seemed like my desires were being denied because of a choice I did not make with my first pregnancy. In January 2002, I must have hit the lottery because I became pregnant again, and this time I was able to carry the baby full term. September 2002, I birthed my second child, and I felt like I was settled because I had my daughter and now my son. Well, that was not it. In 2003 here comes another pregnancy and another miscarriage. I was done! I said to God, *"Why am I going through this? What have I done to deserve all of this? Is it because of the first abortion? Why is my body constantly going through these changes?"* I had all these questions, becoming more and more frustrated and broken. I could not carry something precious to me to full term, and the weight of the loss was too much to bear.

My life was in shambles because I had been through so much mentally and physically. I never really dealt with the issues of loss and shame. I swept them under my pretty rug and left them there to build up. I did not want to ever experience anything else like this. SIX TIMES BEING PREGNANT! I felt like I was being punished because I had not dealt with the things I kept under the rug. But in the seventh and final year I had a full-term pregnancy and baby number three in 2004. It was then that I made the official decision to have my tubes tied because I did not want to become pregnant anymore.

The decision to have an abortion sat with me for a long time. My abortion was a tragedy; one that I did not want and one that needed to be addressed and healed. I was too scared to tell anyone about my abortion because I couldn't believe that I actually did it. I constantly questioned myself, and desperately wanted to bring forth children to show that I could be all that God still wanted me to be as a mother. I could have told others. I could have received support, but I didn't be-cause I was too afraid. I did not open myself up to receive any help that others tried to give during that time either. The guilt and shame of the abortion, and the feelings of being punished through my miscarriages caused me to hide from others. But I knew that I could not give up on myself or throw in the towel. I had to process the pain of loss, grief, guilt, and shame to experience healing.

I finally gained the courage to open up about my seven-year jour-ney dealing with abortion, miscarriages, grief and loss. At the time, my spouse didn't even know about the abortion. When you hide trauma on the inside, it can break you and cause you to feel like something is wrong with you; like you are incomplete. I no longer wanted to feel ashamed of what I had gone through, so I began to share my story. I had to use wisdom in selecting who I shared my story with because you cannot trust everyone with your heart. I built up my confidence in shedding the weight of the guilt and shame and became unafraid of sharing my journey. It took perseverance and resilience to share such a hard journey. I started hanging around like-minded people and received advice that helped me along the way. My boldness to share led to a place of healing and peace.

Sometimes we hide the things that we have been through because of our shame and guilt, and this may prevent us from walking in the things God has for us because we are stagnant and haven't healed. We think about what we want for our lives and not what God wants. When I think about being pregnant and the trimesters that I went through, I also think about it in our natural lives. As leaders, God will take us through many trimesters. During our trimesters things begin to change. I had to heal from my past and not see myself as incomplete or unable to move beyond that space. I had to release and heal from the things that burdened me and move into a different place in life.

As leaders, if we do not heal from our past experiences, we can often mis-carry our mantle, mis-carry the people that we are positioned to lead, and mis-carry the anointing we have in our lives. To be a bold woman and leader, God had to show me that I will not always be perfect, but I can continue to strive for the best of myself. As leaders we will not always get it right, and we may go through many challenges, but it is the understanding that we can recognize those moments when we fumble and correct them. I turned my seven years of tests and trials into seven years of testimony by no longer being afraid and ashamed of my past mistakes and tragedy. I was no longer afraid of my story.

I say to you, do not be afraid to walk and operate in your boldness! Understand that when God says that there is nothing too hard for Him, He means it, because He is not a man that He should lie. You no longer need to be afraid of your past or your past mistakes. Be the person and the leader that GOD has created you to be - for yourself and others - and walk boldly in your journey of healing and freedom!

Reflections

....

....

....

....

....

....

....

....

....

....

....

....

....

....

....

....

....

....

....

....

....

....

....

....

....

Beyond Ordinary Limits – DARING!

BY NICOLE ELLIS

"WE ARE GOING TO WIN." That's what I live every day. I previously made the mistake of focusing on people when I should have focused on how I could serve and lead people while being fully and BOLDLY me. So, I use my bold personality as fuel in my roles as a wife, mother, leader, and entrepreneur. I'm not competitive, but I never run from a challenge. I compete to be the best version of myself. Tell me I can't do it and watch me crush it in first place – no excuses!

When I trace my history, there are many things that contributed to the boldness I embrace today. However, overall, weight was my nemesis. I've struggled with my weight all of my life. From silently struggling with an eating disorder as a teen, to battling morbid obesity as an adult, weight challenges have always lurked around the corner. I've ridden the roller coaster of low self-esteem, surfed the tidal wave of keeping up with man's beauty's standards, and hid behind the masks of being body shamed by family, enemies, friends and even myself. I've been *"pretty for a big girl," "cute for a thick girl,"* and any other variation of shady compliments. If I had to give it a name it's an *"insult-iment."* Trying to juggle the opinions of others began to eat away at my confidence and affected my ability to lead well. I found myself following people for approval and it was taking its toll on me.

In my teens, I was petite, but I loved to eat. After giving birth to my daughter at sixteen, my curves made a grand appearance. **BOOM, BAM, POW!** I was curvy in all the right places, but curves weren't embraced back then. My family loved me; however, their words cut deep when they poked fun at the thickness of my thighs, the roundness of my rump, or the fullness of my face. *"Nikki, you better stop eating your mother's cooking,"* was the statement I heard the most. Jokes about our weight was the norm in the family, but it left hidden scars no one ever spoke about. I remember a childhood saying, *"Sticks and stones may break my bones, but words will never hurt me."* Well, whoever made that up is a LYING WONDER and they should have their lips glued shut. Words are seeds and there were so many negative seeds planted in my life.

It appeared being skinny was synonymous with beauty. Because a healthy diet and exercise wasn't in my plans, anorexia became my secret love affair. My weight dropped drastically, but my curves were accentuated. I was the shape of a Coke bottle in 1998. Some people questioned how small I had gotten, and the catcalls from the guys got louder. I wasn't comfortable in my skin, but I began mastering how to pretend. I learned to make any size work even though the opinions of people were slowly eating away at my soul. Don't get me wrong, I was a *"boss"* even in my youth as a student leader, honor roll student, and activist in my church and community. However, when you don't know who you are or don't fully embrace who you are, it's easy to settle instead of stand out. I settled when God wanted me to stand out.

As I continued to struggle with my weight and self-esteem as a teenage mother, I turned to food for my comfort. When life happened, I ate. When family members died, I ate. When I was struggling as a single mother, pursuing a college degree, and working full-time trying to keep the lights on, I ate. When I was rejected by men, I ate. When I was judged by my family, I ate. When I was stressed out, I ate. Emotional eating became the thing to do. Family and friends made it easy because we ate to celebrate the joys of life, we ate to mourn the loss of loved ones, heck we ate because it was Monday. We all were gaining weight and found comfort in knowing we were all in the same situation. I learned to embrace my body no matter the shape. So, confidence, although manufactured, became the thing I knew how to do. I was bold as the thick girl, big girl, whatever girl. I didn't come to play; I came to slay!

There's a saying, *"You have to fake it till you make it."* Some people reject this premise, but real talk, it was where I began walking in boldness. I like how the Bible says in Romans 4:17b ESV[1] *"[God] calls into existence the things that do not exist".* I had to start speaking to myself about my beauty, my confidence, and my health as though they already existed. I love having bold, colorful hair as much as people love changing their clothes. So, I decided to embrace the creative side of my personality. Bold, bright hair colors. Eccentric clothing. Chunky color jewelry. I started loving myself.

I met my husband when I was thick with fire-engine red hair. He married me when I was fluffy with a short haircut and a lot of butt. I started understanding my confidence wasn't contingent on a *"perfect"* package. My advice to the women reading this is to begin loving yourself for who God created you to be and if you don't like something, change it. I went on to lose nearly ninety pounds between 2011-2013. More confidence was unearthed because I began breaking the barriers my nemesis had built around me. I was able to see ME for the first time in a long time. My nemesis showed up in 2014 as postpartum weight gain after my third baby. I ate because I was nursing. I ate because I earned it; as it was my third baby, somebody better run me my fried chicken and fries. Between 2013-2020, I gained 108.3 disrespectful

---

1. *The Holy Bible, English Standard Version. ESV® Text Edition: 2016. Copyright © 2001 by Crossway Bibles, a publishing ministry of Good News Publishers.*

pounds. Why didn't someone stop me; heck, why didn't I stop myself? I was heading for a sea of health issues if I didn't make some changes. I feared continuing the cycle of death due to complications with weight related illnesses. High blood pressure, heart disease, and diabetes runs in my family. And unfortunately, I lost my father and grandmother due to health issues. I do not want these things in my life. I have to live for myself and my family.

Overcoming one challenge in life doesn't mean you will never encounter it again. Sometimes it will come dressed up in a different suit causing the same trouble. I was now a wife, a mother three times over, a coach, an employee, and an entrepreneur. And I was still being attacked. *"GOD, HELP ME!"* This was my plea. I was so sick of how I was feeling, I wanted to get back to me. Not the me that used to pretend, but the me who embraced the beauty within. God answered my prayers and gave me a jumpstart. Correction, He catapulted me forward, but it required work. I dropped 112.7lbs in nine months through fitness and diet changes and I'm not going back. I'm a bold black woman with a fiery red fade with designs on the side. I'm BOLD. Beyond Ordinary Limits. **DARING!** My father would be proud of me.

I am BOLD and guess what? You are BOLD too! You have to call those things that do not exist into existence. Remember God created you, so you are not a mistake. You are fearfully and wonderfully made (Psalm 139:14 ESV). If you want to go to a new level, take the limits off of yourself. Man does not define you. God does. You have to first decide that you are sick and tired of your circumstance and you want to do the work to change it. Your why has to be so strong that it overcomes all of your excuses. If you're not already doing what is required then rethink your why. You may have setbacks, but never quit. Find that one thing that makes your heart soar. Do you have it? Now keep that in front of you at all times. When people see you, let them see the you GOD sees. And while you may not be where you want to be, you can embrace where you are today.

The lessons I learned through my journey helped me to walk in my boldness. I am able to minister to people from all walks of life. I exude the light of Christ with a lioness boldness. When you fully embrace who you are, the walls come down and people will be drawn to the light inside of you. So, roar, Lioness, roar! Go forth and be BOLD!

Reflections

....

....

....

....

....

....

....

....

....

....

....

....

....

....

....

....

....

....

....

....

....

I AM
AUTHENTIC

"The lioness's roar has a distinct sound that cannot be duplicated. Your voice is unique, and no one can recreate it."

Dr. Synetheia

The Lioness Leads Authentically

AUTHENTICITY HAS BECOME UNDERRATED. The value of being honest, trustworthy, and genuine has been lost in a societal and governmental culture that seems to honor deceit and duplication. Today, we are surrounded by messaging that produces a climate of vicious comparison, whether in our appearance, credentials, or material assets. Yet authenticity is of great value and great need. Authenticity reflects honesty and truth not only in our words but also in our actions. Authenticity is a celebration of the original, unique purpose of a person or thing; it is the uncompromised version. When we reject the comparison game and choose authenticity as a way of life, we embrace our uniqueness. Also, it is a statement that who our Creator made was not an accident nor a coincidence. Instead, each of us was thoughtfully, intentionally, and strategically created with a distinct purpose. No matter the circumstances under which we arrived in the world, we are not accidents. We are authentic creations.

Fear sends messaging suggesting that if we don't act or think like others, we are wrong. Fear suggests that we are not good enough in our original state and that we must work overtime to catch up to the standards of others. Authenticity silences the voice of fear. Each time we choose to show up with our quirkiness, and our unique line-up of gifts, talents, and abilities, we choose authenticity.

Much like how a lioness never pretends to be a tiger, you should never choose to be anyone except who you were created to be. Though tigers and lionesses are in the same feline family, they are not the same and they were not meant to be the same. You were not meant to be anyone other than _____ (insert your name here). The lioness's prowl may share some common themes as the tiger, but her prowl is so much more calculating and patient. The lioness's roar has a distinct sound that cannot be duplicated. Your voice is unique, and no one can recreate it.

As a woman who leads, when you have a seat at the table, people need to hear your voice, your thoughts, and your ideas. Fear tells us that our voice is not required nor wanted. Fear tells us that our way will never be accepted. Yet the woman who shows up authentically makes a bold statement to fear that its opinions are not needed or wanted! The woman who shows up authentically doesn't need permission to be herself. She knows the value she carries, and it increases her confidence and courage. The authentic woman knows that ten thousand people in a room may be capable of executing the same task, but no one can ever do it the way she does it! Authenticity is a slap in the face of our spiritual enemy. He is a master deceiver and manipulator of truth, specializing in being disingenuous. And when we choose to show up as anything less than who our Creator made us to be, we are aligning with the lies of our spiritual enemy and telling our Creator that what He made us to be is insufficient. As leaders, those who follow us need us to bring our best and authentic selves into what we do. We possess something they need. We will not disappoint!

THE LIONESS LEADS AUTHENTICALLY

Today, we choose to be women who embrace this truth: "I am enough."

We are uniquely and intentionally created.
We reject all comparisons to other people and recognize we are valuable just as we are.
We choose to show up and use our voices without compromise.
We choose authenticity over pretense.

Lead "You"niquely

BY SHENAY LEWIS-HAIRSTON

I HAVE WORKED IN SECTORS of non-profit, state government, school systems, and healthcare. As diverse as my careers have been, one thing I have faced at each level was conforming to fit *"their"* rules. I felt I had to fit into this polished, posed, and pristine look to advance my career, when in fact I was the total opposite of that *"look."* My world consisted of color and vibrance, not a black and white existence, and when it comes to leadership, sometimes that can be too fine of a line to walk.

In 2005 I was working for the government and our department offered me a fringe benefit of going into the local school system to participate in a Read Out Loud initiative. When I was asked to participate, I was overly excited because I had so many ideas for stories that I wanted to read to the children. I had my reading rainbow party already planned out in my head, and I was excited to partake in this event. I was given instructions to read one book to three different classes, get in and out of the classroom, and most importantly, do nothing fancy. I did exactly as I was asked and went into the school as a plain, government official with a book. Needless to say, the event was a disaster.

The children were not attentive to me reading to them on the first day of Read Out Loud. The teachers apologized and even tried to rally the children to listen. I was so defeated after leaving that school that I wanted to remove my name from the list of volunteers. As the weeks passed, that one event replayed in my mind repeatedly. I knew I could have made that event fun and memorable, but I didn't because I conformed to what others wanted for the event. My coworkers encouraged me to go back and do what I thought would work, and in true form I debated with myself about what I should do. Do I continue on this dismal path with inattentive children, or do I strip off my government role for the real me? I decided that I would do it my way. I arrived at the school dressed like the main character in the book. I was fancy! Immediately, from the time I walked into the classroom until I finished the story, the children were attentive and excited. After reading time was over, one of the students could not wait to share her overwhelming excitement for the book and my costume.

As I drove home that night, I reflected on how I allowed the unofficial rules of one department to compromise my creativity. Instead of taking a stand and voicing my unique thoughts, my insecurities dictated a negative outcome. Why would I quiet my uniqueness when that is the only way I know how to be in life? I needed to just be myself. Once I made the conscious decision to execute my plan for the reading event, the results were effectively received.

So, I held on to that thinking as I transitioned into my next position in the healthcare system. I was twenty-six when I entered the healthcare world, and although I was proving to myself that being authentic was the right choice, I was still learning how to use my authenticity in different settings. What I realized was I had become what the in-crowd wanted me to be because it was comfortable for others and kept the world at bay. To prove this point, I thought this new job was the place for me. I was tucked away in the basement, only coming up to see patients when absolutely necessary. I stayed hidden to cover my, as others might say, 'over-the-top' personality. My boss, a micromanager who needed to control every aspect of the staff's daily work schedule, shifted more responsibilities my way that were outside of my job description. I said nothing. He established our break times and even installed cameras to watch the employees. I started to feel like a hamster in a cage, waiting on the consequences of a wrong move or action.

Staff members began complaining about the rules and how our boss's decisions made them feel uncomfortable. As time passed, the conditions worsened to the point that the boss was terminated. During that time of transition, I was forced to the foreground to become a leader over my section. In ten years, I saw many things that were not right, yet I said nothing because I didn't want to be the odd ball. An interim director was hired to lead until a permanent director could be found. The interim director then sat down with each of us to get a better understanding of our office. While meeting with the director, she asked why I thought the office was in the condition it was in. I discussed a couple of concerns and issues with her only to be asked what can be done to fix it. I had no answer to offer her. How could I speak my mind when I've been hiding it for so long? What would they think? How would they react? Playing it safe was a norm for me in this role, so why would I change now? In that moment, I remembered that experience years earlier where I let rules compromise who I was and the authentic ideas I had to correct the problems. It was manifesting in both my professional and spiritual life, and a change needed to come sooner than later.

I struggled with my insecurities of hiding my authenticity for fear of others' opinions. Not only was I dealing with living authentically at work, but at that time God was also calling me into ministry. I was walking out the realistic life of Jonah, running as far away as possible. God dealt with me for over a year as I ran further and further from Him and my calling. I wanted to stay tucked away from everything; my authenticity would be too much for others to handle. My life was full of color, glitter, sparkle, and unicorns. Life was too black and white, and I wanted to liven it up with me.

I started to pay closer attention to this struggle when I was in the hospital after an organ was removed. I journal often, and I realized that whenever I conformed, I didn't meet my goals. But every time I was my authentic self, my goals were met. During that time of healing, I surrendered my YES to preaching the gospel. Surrendering my yes to my calling also surrendered my yes for my assignment at work. When I returned to work, I requested a meeting with my interim director to render my honest opinions and solutions. The director asked why I never spoke about or implemented any of my ideas, and I explained that I felt they were so wild and extraordinary, I feared that people would judge me or call me a weirdo. At times, my ideas are so far-fetched that I almost can't believe it myself. My director encouraged me to take two of my solutions and implement them no matter how many people supported me. I implemented the two ideas, and they were wild enough that they actually worked!

I learned that being my authentic self has opened up many opportunities to lead and serve others in ministry and at work. Learning to be authentic did not happen overnight and there are days that I still struggle with it. However, the difference now is that when I feel myself conforming to how the world expects me to be, I stop and remember I am uniquely created in His image. I am tired of people pleasing and I am only concerned with pleasing God. He created me to be different and I know my God does not make any mistakes. So, yes, I may show up with purple hair at work, and put a troll and unicorn on my desk. Yes, I may show up with some type of flashing head band on for a holiday party. Yes, I may show up wearing Chucks and a skirt to preach; maybe even a crown. The greatest gift I can give God is to just show up being exactly who He created and needs me to be for myself and others.

If I could leave you with anything it would be my six daily leadership principles:

1. Live to make a DIFFERENCE in your life and in the lives of others.

2. Believe in helping others SUCCEED.
3. LEAD by example.
4. Understand that HELPING others succeed is the key to your own success.
5. MOTIVATE yourself and do everything in your power to INSPIRE you.
6. I am on a GOD SIZE assignment.

Remember to Live and Lead "You"niquely! Your uniqueness is needed in this world.

Reflections

....

....

....

....

....

....

....

....

....

....

....

....

....

....

....

....

....

....

....

....

Show Up
BY CHARLA ARMSTEAD

AS MOST LEADERS, I am not immune to struggling with fear while having full awareness of my authentic, God given gifts and purpose. I was often told by my parents and teachers that I was born to be a leader. In fact, some of my earliest memories are of me giving directions on the playground of how and what *"we"* were going to play. Yet, as time progressed the innocence of the playground gave way to my personal, college, ministry, and work relationships that were not always amenable to my self-proclaimed *"brilliant"* ideas. As I developed in these new spaces of leadership, I had to learn to adjust to a spectrum of others' experiences with me; from slight opposition of my ideas to blatant rejection. We all have faced some level of resistance in life. However, it deals the most harrowing blows when it comes from toxic leadership and relationships. After enough bumps and bruises, we sometimes begin to walk with a limp. I was dealing with these blows in both my personal and professional life, which caused me to change who I had been in my prior years. My experience with this toxicity transformed this once brave, bold, courageous little girl into a more cautious, check the box, rule abiding adult. In these atmospheres, I began walking on eggshells to keep the peace, no longer showing up as my authentic self.

Fear and self-doubt emerged as I held in tandem my innate gifts, acquired skills, and the conflicting ideas of remaining in good graces with people in authority. Navigating multiple realities and mixed messages came with a sobering reality. Some people will love your authentic gift when it works to build their goals and glorify them. At the same time, they may also abhor it when your authenticity exposes the counterfeits they present to the world. Your very existence arouses their own internal conflict, and you now become something that needs to be controlled by them. These decisions to control me became especially daunting when they weighed not only on my leadership values, but tempted me to compromise my core values, too. I tried my best to walk in both worlds, trying to understand the person and the reasons behind the decisions, while firmly advocating for things that benefited the affected staff.

It is hard to work in an environment, let alone walk in a position of leadership, when authority figures lack understanding, empathy, and support of their staff. I'm reminded of one occasion when tragedy struck my workplace. A key leader in our building suffered a tragic, unexpected death. This woman was poised, seasoned, and revered. Thought of by many as the heartbeat of our workplace, her death reverberated among our institution of learning at deafening decibels. The weight of the loss left a gaping hole in more ways than one, unearthing great conflict that had been brewing under the surface for years. High levels of leadership felt the weight of achieving high test scores, administrative compliance, and finishing the year strong. It was a sense of urgency to fill her empty role and get back to *"business."* Unfortunately, this approach towards a staff that already felt overworked, undervalued, and underappreciated, was ill received. It implied that their pain over the loss of one of their leaders did not matter, and they needed to simply move forward and get back to work. Colleagues cried out for a space to mourn a life that had an indelible impact on them beyond her role and function. Although I had no direct authority over my colleagues, I was sought out as a leader by both my peers and those in authority to help in this situation. Meetings were endless, tears were shed in private, *"Can I talk to you?"* moments were innumerable, and my God consciousness was being pricked daily. I created a space for others to privately mourn when a public space was urgently needed.

Do I risk presenting *"doing the right thing"* to a leader who has a tendency for backlash and retaliation when someone does not line up with what the leader feels is the priority? After all, my role in the building was by invitation and not guaranteed. I was not covered by a license, contract, or union. Do I allow my take-charge, bold, authentic self to finally speak up? Or do I allow others to suffer silently, which I knew in my heart would ultimately tear against the fabric of our workplace in deeply devastating ways? I know that I am called to advocate for the voiceless and vulnerable, the unseen, the left out and the forgotten. I'm not one to sit by and watch others in pain and not speak up or work to relieve it. At times, this has threatened my own personal comfort or secure status. But to not speak up would be inauthentic, to say the least. I knew what it was like to be free to voice my feelings and to be myself. I also knew what it was like to feel voiceless, stifled, and helpless. I saw this happening in this moment and I did not want to stand by the wayside and do nothing. I did not want to look back on my life and regret not taking the opportunity to walk in my true authenticity; something I needed to get back to no matter whose eggshells I cracked.

Recently, on my daily walk, I looked up into the sky and noticed three birds and airplanes flying at the same time. Their differing characteristics were very distinct. The planes flew one fixed direction and pattern. I was keenly aware that any changes in their set course requires major communication with the tower and permission to change course or altitudes. Their vision is limited to technology and aeronautical estimations based on theories and best practices. There was a stark contrast of the birds. Their flight was free, unassuming, and unbothered by seemingly close neighbors in the heavenlies. They could fly in circles and in close proximity to one another. Seemingly, they demonstrated great freedom simply doing what they were created to do. They are the original. Airplanes are more massive, a viable tool, and definitely more expensive, yet as a created thing, limited in so many ways.

I never observed birds trying to be a plane. It appeared that these animals discovered something we continue to try to figure out: being true to what you are called and created to be. Authenticity means operating in and by God's original design for you, not as a manmade duplication limited in function. After much prayer, I took the risk of approaching our leader. I went in, knees shaking with full knowledge that this could elicit retribution. By the hand of God, she conceded and gave our team free reign to coordinate a celebration of life that included colleagues, students, parents and even the broader community. I stood up for what was right for the staff, and I knew then that I could also continue to stand up for myself by continuing to remember my authentic and God given gifts and purpose. I needed to walk in the freedom of authenticity I once had because it was what I was destined to do.

Learning to counter our fears to show up authentically is not always easy. I first had to have faith to believe that who God has authentically called and created me to be is valuable and necessary. I had to remember that I'm more resilient, strong, and capable than what I had become when I changed for others. Despite how grandiose any opposing forces present themselves against me, they pale in comparison to the great I AM. I was created to be exactly who I am, and when I let go of that identity, I let go of myself.

I had to pull on the strength and experience of mentors, team members, and intercessors with similar values to get back to my authentic self. It is essential that these people in your circle are identified wisely and tried over various seasons. They are a source of accountability; guideposts when I lose my way. I could voice my opinions, share my boldness, and speak and live freely in these safe spaces. The benefit of being surrounded by people who remind me of who I am and whose I am is inexplicable.

Lastly, I have learned irreplaceable lessons through failure and recovery. Living authentically is not always welcomed. It has cost me relationships, community standing, financial resources and positions of favor. Some days, I shudder at the losses. In one season, it haunted me, until I took account of all I have gained in coming home to my authentic self. The tradeoff of peace, clarity, renewed purpose, and abundant joy is immeasurable. Your flight in life will be more liberating when you remain your authentic self.

Reflections

....

....

....

....

....

....

....

....

....

....

....

....

....

....

The Rhythm
of Freedom

BY RASHEENA HARRIS

MY HUSBAND AND I met at the group home where our love affair with community work and empowering young people began. He was a homebound instructor for a young man who had been there for seven months and was heavily into gang life before his placement. His father was a prominent pastor and activist. His mother passed way too soon after we began seeing one another. She was well respected, admired and missed by congregations across the local area.

We began dating and were engaged two years into the relationship. At the time, I had two jobs: to "save the world" by day, and "party and chill" by night. To me it was the best of both worlds and I loved every minute of it. My husband visited me once at the strip club where I bartended. He said he could not come back because of who he was and what his family represented. He proposed. We married. And then he had a conversation with me that changed everything.

He indicated that he had been called to ministry and that I would have to quit bartending. But that was not the only thing that changed. That was just the beginning. He was the ying to my yang, the calm to my storm and it worked really well…until it didn't.

There was an expectation for how the change was supposed to go. A title and position. A wonderful church welcome and acceptance. A belonging and sense of tribe. But none of that happened. I was me, but I was told I couldn't be me anymore. Me wasn't enough. But, why? We were always opposites, connected by our passion in our work, our leadership, and our heart for people. He married me – I was enough. Why am I not accepted in OUR church? I was disappointed. I felt rejected, confused, and alone. I allowed these circumstances to change me. Abandoned to the background of my husband's calling and career, I left my own aspirations on the back burner. I went into myself, peering out into this world with questioning eyes.

Dear Lady Loneliness,

They made me cry again today. They don't even know me. They don't know my heart, my visions, my goals. It's maddening and infuriating that these church folks won't give me a chance. I told the choir director that I could not make it to practice early on Saturdays because I get off at 3am. After working the bar, doing inventory, and counting my drawer I'm typically exhausted. I guess I was supposed to come up with a more appropriate lie, so as to not make people uncomfortable. Or maybe I should have told them that some of their deacons keep me occupied most of the night with stories of being bored and unhappy at home.

I felt invisible. If I can be honest, I was often forgotten. Sometimes while visiting a church, my husband managed to work through his nerves enough to mention me. It's an awkward feeling. It's like I wasn't even there. I always had to have my guard up. I didn't know who genuinely wanted to support me or who just wanted to get closer to him. They watch everything. How I sit, what I wear, how I respond. I'm constantly wondering who my real friends are. I had no true relationships. I'm an outcast and on my own, always taking a back seat. My interactions change because of my husband's status—a lot changes. The expectation is that I change because I am a minister's wife. I try to please everyone but myself. Many times, I silently asked myself, "What about me?"

THE RHYTHM OF FREEDOM

I used to model before I met him. I went to Caribbean Clubs. I didn't go to church much. I was married to my career and planned to work my way up the corporate ladder. I was strong, resilient and driven. I was raised by my Caribbean parents and my dominant, assertive, and direct Barbadian-Guyanese mother, who came from a long lineage of independent women. If I am not careful, I will completely lose my way. Lose my fire. Lose myself.

So down here I am given the unofficial title of First Lady. If it's something official I'm supposed to be beside him. Like a silent partner. With the new age I don't have to necessarily match, but it's better to compliment. Other times, most times, I'm disposable. Simply there with no direction. Ninety percent of the time I have no role because I am alone. That's a sad thing but it's the truth. It's just me and God.

He often cheats on me with the church. I learn the life of being a single mother quickly because of his other obligations that take away his time and attention. He may be away on a conference and I will have to send video and pictures of recitals and competitions. And the expectation is that I take it like a champ. Play the part and look poised and happy while doing it even if my heart is slowly breaking. Being the Type-A that I am, I had to create my role as time went on. I considered myself his administrator, protector, filter, and organizer of all things. I like to call myself his supporting actress. I was a manager-in-training while losing ground and so desperately wanting to be content and fulfilled.

I decided to say and do something. In my background roles, I was often approached by other women who were like me – authentic. I was waiting for my turn to go for my goals. I decided that I wanted a new career. I decided that I didn't want to do life feeling alone. I decided that I was done with the facade and that I wanted to live the life I had always imagined on purpose and in my truth.

Now Lady Loneliness, I don't have the grand equation as to when this moment will come for you. I don't know what circumstances will lead to your transition. But I know a man who does.

My father-in-love gave me a book several years ago about a woman who had a prayer box. Her prayer boxes were found by her children after her passing. It held hundreds of prayers that she had written throughout her lifetime. They were written on all kinds of scraps of paper, all colors, even napkins. I was so moved that I went to the store and purchased a small $2.00 decorative gift box with a lid. For the past five years, I have had my prayer box. The only rules were to pray whenever led and once I drop the prayer in the box, I give it totally to God. The first night I wrote eighteen prayers. I wrote prayers for myself, our marriage, our family, and our church. My hands were tired of writing, but my heart felt so light. There was a release that night and many days after. My added prayer is that your release will come too.

Sincerely,

The First Lady

There are other Lady Loneliness' out there who know what this, or something similar to this, feels like. They know the pain and struggle I endured, leaving my authentic self for *"greener pastures."* You are not alone. You, exactly as you are, are valued, and there is a way back to your true authenticity. The journey back to myself started when women in the church would cautiously approach me for conversation, support, and encouragement. They would often say things like, *"You're real," "You're not judgmental," "I like how direct you are,"* and that gave me my aha moment. I realized there is something to me just being me. I am not traditional, so why would I think that my life as a first lady would be that way? My purpose is to engage in non-traditional ministry so that I can minister to nontraditional women. Women who also belonged in the group but had different views and needs, like me. That was my calling, and when I began to walk in it, my life completely changed.

I was authentic before I became a first lady and supporter of my husband's ministry and career goals. And making the decision to refine my authenticity in my new role gave me the confidence and strength to act and take MY life back. No longer do I hide my authentic personality, culture, and cultivated gifts. I use them now to not only support and sustain my family, but to minister to women, and push for my own goals and endeavors. Your winning season will arise and give way to the life you envisioned for yourself. Refresh your life to be authentically you. Find in your heart the rhythm of freedom that leads you to never feel lonely again. And always remember that God has created this space in life just for you. Always walk in your authenticity.

Reflections

....

....

....

....

....

....

....

....

....

....

....

....

....

....

....

....

....

....

I AM
COURAGEOUS

"Courage is not the absence of fear. Courage is experiencing anxiety and choosing to confront it and move forward."

Dr. Synetheia

The
Lioness
Leads
Courageously

THERE ARE SO MANY THINGS and people that can evoke fear in us. Everyone has something or someone they fear. For many, fear has been a constant in their lives for years. It is a regular companion that often talks us out of trying new things, taking risks, and exploring new opportunities. As women who lead, especially in places dominated by men, fear tells us that we don't measure up. Fear also whispers that we don't have a right to be at the table. Fear may even lie and tell us that we lack the credentials needed to make a difference. It is in moments of fear that we must be courageous.

Courage is not the absence of fear. Courage is experiencing anxiety and choosing to confront it and move forward. Courage stretches us beyond our comfort zones and challenges us to be adventurous, to persevere, and to face difficulty head-on. Like the lioness, courage fights. The lioness is one of the most courageous creations God made. As the backbone of the pride, the lioness must go out each day to secure food for the cubs, other lionesses, and lions. She knows the risk. She's aware of the plausibility of defeat from a pack of hyenas. She knows that encountering a pit of poisonous snakes could destroy her. Yet, the value and importance of reaching the goal drives her and causes her to show up, when hiding would be a reasonable option. It's scary out there in the darkness of night, lying in wait for her prey, yet the lioness remains hunkered down, awaiting the right time to strike. The woman who leads must exhibit the same type of courage.

There are snakes in the workplace and packs of hyenas in ministry and on the entrepreneurial landscape. Yet, the woman who leads acknowledges the fear and chooses to confront and advance. Those who follow her and rely on her leadership are counting on her courage to succeed. The courageous woman is resilient too. When she heads out into battle, she gets battered sometimes, and everything in her says, "Retreat and don't go back." Yet courage screams, "I WILL ADVANCE!"

We are courageous.
We confront and advance.
We feel the fear and move anyway.
We choose courage over fear.

The Water Didn't Overtake Me

BY KIESHENNA MABRY

IT WAS A SUNDAY NIGHT and there was a hard knock at the door. I wasn't expecting anyone; besides, all three of my sons were now settled into their dorms. Fall semester was due to start the next day, and I had talked with my oldest son before falling asleep. We ended our conversation as usual with *"Lovebye."* That was our cute love language whenever we ended a call. I peeped out the door to see who it could be. There stood two detectives. *"Can I help you?"* I asked in a very disturbed tone. *"Are you Kieshenna?"* one of the detectives asked. *"Yes, I AM!"* The officers flashed their badges as one said, *"We are from the Norfolk Police Department and we would like to speak with you."* When I heard the word Norfolk, I got a little nervous because my oldest son attended Norfolk State University. I immediately started thinking what he could have done to get himself in trouble, which would have been totally out of character for him.

As a boy mom, as they like to call it now, I lead my household in a very authoritative manner; but once children become adults, they are totally responsible for the choices they make. I was very apprehensive about letting the officers in. Fearful to hear what he had done to break the law. All I know is that it must have been pretty bad for the detectives to be sitting in my living room on a late Sunday night. They asked if I knew Jae Mabry. *"Yes, he's my son."* The detective stared at me with a blank stare. At this point my stomach began to sink. I knew before he opened his mouth that it was bad. *"Do you know Jaequan?"* he said. *"Listen, sir, yes!"* I said, pointing to the family portrait of me and my sons. *"Ms. Mabry, I am sorry. He passed away tonight."* I sat and stared at him momentarily before I began to scream hysterically. I tried to stand but my body became limp. Between screams I tried to remember my mother's phone number as they were trying to call. *"We have come to take you to identify him."*

As I sat in the back of the detectives' car with my mother, I recall my body being numb. I began to reflect on his life and think no, not my first-born son. My twenty-three-year-old son, a senior in college, was gone. I wish I could make the entire scenario make sense. He loved water and could swim very well, but somehow my baby had accidentally drowned. Between the currents and it being dark, he struggled. I was told he was yelling for help when he started to struggle. I thought, *"How could I let him down?"* Yes, me, his mother. I was not there but somehow, I held myself totally responsible. He was yelling for his mother and of all times when he needed me the most, I was not there and his life depended on it. Processing that is a crippling pain that I still face to this day and probably will for the rest of my life.

Jae's birth was just as traumatic as his death. It was really quiet in the maternity ward until I started screaming like I was in a horror movie. Within minutes of my roar, I gave birth to my first-born son. At the tender age of fifteen, I became a mother. Being fifteen with a baby and no clue about life was traumatic. By the age of nineteen, I was the mother of three boys. Statistically, the odds were stacked against me and my three sons. As a single, young mom of three boys, many watched in anticipation of my failure. Life was difficult, and it took a lot of courage and fight in me to be the best mother I could be for them. I struggled internally. The judgments of others left me in constant attack mode, causing me to struggle with anxiety and depression. Feelings of inadequacy and fear that I would fail as a mother and cause my sons to fail plagued me. As the saying goes, *"The struggle was real!"*

When my sons were young, they didn't understand what I was going through. I had plans to become a nurse, and I knew I had to juggle many responsibilities to make that happen. So, I'd get off work, go to school, pick up the kids, take them to their sports practices, and take care of them while handling work and school. I struggled financially and always felt like a failure because I couldn't give my kids everything I wanted them to have for their success. I suppressed my internal feelings so my children wouldn't know what I was going through. I kept pushing, some days not even wanting to get out of bed and face the next day. But I didn't have a choice because "the boys," as I would often refer to them, needed me. My sons were my life. As adults they described me as being mean and strict when they were younger. What they did not understand was that I was protecting them. I wanted them to have every opportunity that was afforded to them, and I didn't want them, or me, to become the negative statistics that everyone thought we would be. People would often tell me I was doing a great job raising the boys, but deep down inside I felt like I was not doing enough. I felt inadequate. The invisible enemy of fear is not of God. I was pushing them to have goals while at the same time talking myself out of obtaining my own because I did not feel that I was good enough. When I did not get accepted into a nursing program, I was devastated. I felt like I would never reach my goals and I gave up on that particular dream. I didn't give myself credit for the many other things that I had accomplished. Although I did not become a nurse at that time, I worked in healthcare for years while raising successful and strong young men. I was a leader as a mother, and a leader in life in showing how I overcame obstacles.

If I told you that life was perfect now, I would be lying. As life started to change and my boys were now young men, it did my heart good to see them all head off to college. But one life changing event left me on the floor in a fetal position crying at night. Asking God, *"Why did this happen to me?"* My heart was broken beyond repair. Although my sons were young adults, they still needed me. They needed me now more than ever. And my grief is like the weather in March, I never know what to expect. I had just launched my business as an event planner when my son died, and somehow, I still had to lead in my business. I funeralized my son one day and the next day, I coordinated a wedding. I had to find the strength and resilience to continue on that day. The same strength and resilience I instilled in my boys had to be instilled in myself, too. That took courage.

There were times as a leader when I had to STAND even when I wanted to hide and not face the next day. I continue on while I am living out the scripture 2 Corinthians 12:9b (ESV)[1] knowing, *"His power is made perfect in weakness."* Every day is a different emotion, and I have to be honest and say that life has to go on. My life has to keep going without my friend, my son, the one I grew up with, my personal comedian. The hymn, *"Hold to God's Unchanging Hand"* has carried me many days and late in the midnight hour. I'm surviving this current called life. Just as I always tried to lead and guide my sons to be the best they could be, I am now encouraging myself to live a more abundant life.

Be encouraged and know that you can still show up as a courageous leader even through loss. Grief is a process. A painful and necessary process. My son always encouraged me to pursue my dreams wholeheartedly. I not only cheered for my sons, but they cheered and are cheering now for me as well. And now it's time I cheer for myself, too.

I offer these tips to help you on your journey:

1. Strengthen your relationship spiritually to help you through the hardest of times.
2. Surround yourself with a support system who will be there when you need them.

---

1. *The Holy Bible, English Standard Version. ESV® Text Edition: 2016. Copyright © 2001 by <u>Crossway Bibles, a publishing ministry of Good News Publishers</u>.*

3. Seek support for your mental health and get the care and support you need.
4. Try new things.
5. Go after your unfulfilled dreams.

You have the courage to get all you need to move forward in life. If I can walk courageously, so can you.

Reflections

....

....

....

....

....

....

....

....

....

I Traded My Superwoman Cape for Courage

BY COURTNEY GRIFFIN

THE SOUND OF FANTASIA'S soulful voice wafting through the air, *"But what would you be without me? What would you be without me? So what? You blowing up just a little, they knowing you a little, don't give a finger in the middle 'cause you would never be without me."* I dance wildly around my bedroom with the door wide open, fist pumping in the air, loudly and passionately singing as my husband walks through the door. I want him to hear me, to see me as he walks to our guest room to put his things down. I've been watching him sit in the parking lot on his phone for the last hour. That's where he's been spending much of his free time – in his car. My voice oscillates between rich-toned singing and gut-wrenching sobs. It had been three weeks since he calmly told me he no longer wanted to be married. I thought I was a good wife. Not perfect, but good. I worked three jobs while completing my degree to support us when things hadn't gone as planned. I jumped right in and handled it because I could. I didn't complain; to me he was worth it, we were worth it. I blasted my playlist daily. It was a mix of angry, womanist break-up anthems and soul stirring gospel and Christian music ballads. I wanted God to hear me and to intervene, to make him love me again. I wanted my husband to hear my sobs; I wanted him to know he was breaking my heart! It had been three weeks since I called my dad and told him that my husband secured a place to stay six months prior to his announcement, and I had nowhere to go. My dad asked me to leave the life I'd known for the last eleven years and come home. My life was filled with grief. It had been a year and two months since my mother's death and a year since my journey to parenthood through in vitro fertilization had unsuccessfully come to an end. I was alone. I felt as if I was living under water.

Not only was I a wife not wanting to leave my home and marriage, but I was also a leader on my job who had to find the courage to show up and lead a team of wonderful, talented sales associates. Ironically, the company I was working for was also in the process of its own organizational and functional changes. Positions were eliminated, merged, and given to a new set of leaders. I was one of those new leaders to garner a promotion. I had accomplished a goal I'd worked hard to achieve for almost four years, yet the rest of my life was falling apart around me. Being at work became the only time I wasn't crying. For nine hours I could encourage and motivate the team, be a resource for customers, and a brand ambassador for the company. I had no time to grieve. I was courageous at work because I had a job to do and people and tasks to take care of throughout the day. However, once the store was recovered and the doors were locked, I had to go back to reality.

In November 2013 I moved in with my best friend, who is more my sister than friend, until I relocated to my father's house in North Carolina. I slept in her four-year-old daughter's bedroom. Such a beautiful little room; such joy, such innocent hope. Then there were my four black bags piled in the corner. At night I'd lay in bed looking at my belongings stacked in the corner of what was once a perfect little pink room. Sometimes her daughter, who I consider my niece, would get into bed with me and wrap her little arms around my neck and pat my back. I'd lay there with streams of tears running backward from my eyes, creating puddles on the pillow until we both fell asleep or her mom would come and get her. God never left me alone, but that is all I felt – alone. And angry. And afraid. During the loneliest moments, the perfect song began to play in my mind, *"I'm so confused, I know I heard you loud and clear. So, I followed through, somehow I ended up here... All I got is hurt and these four words..."* As the chorus began, I'd silently scream in pain and sing along through rivers of tears, *"Thy - will - be - done."* I didn't understand what was happening, but I trusted that God was in it. He had to be. The day came and I was leaving it all behind! December 2013, I said good-bye! I bid farewell to my co-workers and honestly, not too many others. I never wanted to leave Virginia, but now all I wanted was a new start.

The new journey was paved with great triumph and additional losses. In 2014 I was elevated in ministry and landed a well-paying administrative position. In June of that same year my father died of cancer. We didn't have long to say goodbye; a little over two weeks after the diagnosis he was gone. From his hospital bed he told me to take care of my siblings. I dreaded the weight of that responsibility, but I did it anyway. Little did he know the following year my brother would be diagnosed with congestive heart failure and my sister with multiple sclerosis. I was overwhelmed as executor of my father's estate, helping my siblings and their families, and still trying to prove my worth to a man who'd long decided that he didn't want to be married. I wanted to fall apart, but I couldn't. I was used to keeping it together. Used to handling a situation. I was used to being "perfect"- a superwoman. I was afraid of who I'd be if I couldn't hold it together and be superwoman. So, I held myself together. I didn't have my husband or my parents, and my siblings were counting on me. Who could be there for me – but me?

In the Spring of 2015, I became aware that being superwoman was increasingly difficult. Even superwoman has a vulnerable side. I remember asking God what he wanted from me! What was I missing?

Then, the answer came. *"Seminary. Enroll in seminary."* Why!? Then God brought back a distant memory. Twelve years prior my pastor expressed a desire for me to attend seminary with full endorsement from the church. I left his office rejecting his idea because I was too afraid I'd fail. I didn't believe I was good enough. I didn't want to disappoint him if I failed. So, mustering the courage this time, I enrolled. The following year, I decided to no longer be a convenience to my husband. I let go of the fear of being alone, and after much prayer, I filed for divorce.

During seminary I felt God leading me into chaplaincy, so I changed my concentration and followed God's lead. In 2017, I began to hear God say, *"Go."* How could I just go? Where? I had my parent's house, ministry responsibilities, my job was great, and my siblings needed me. But I felt such a strong urgency to *"go."* That fall I entered a six-month chaplaincy internship which required me to take a deep pay cut from my job. I could no longer afford my mortgage, so I relinquished my home. I let go of anything that didn't fit in my small apartment. Yet, I found my calling, and God confirmed it. One night after I preached at a local church, I had a chance meeting with a Chaplain Resident. After a long conversation with her, I stepped out on faith and applied to three chaplaincy residency programs. I was accepted by hospitals in Florida and Texas. I chose Florida. In August of 2018, I pressed through the fear of the unknown, and with one hundred and fifty dollars to my name, I moved to Jacksonville, Florida.

Residency was challenging and frightening and I battled the desire to quit. But pressing through was greatly rewarding! Immediately following residency, I was hired as a chaplain. Now, I have the opportunity to help patients and their families' journey through their fears into courage and hope. Through each transition, I had to work through my fears. The fear of being alone, disappointing others, not being able to handle it all, and the fear of change. I had to choose to take courageous steps each time. Courage is not the absence of fear, it is simply the choices you make to keep going in the face of it. I am not Superwoman. But

I am a super woman! Overcoming my fears to pursue my true calling helped me move into a place of courage. I hope that in your transitions in life you, too, choose courage over fear.

Reflections

....

....

....

....

....

....

....

....

....

....

....

....

....

....

....

....

....

....

....

....

....

....

Behind
the Scenes

BY HOPE L. HARPER

AS A LEADER, one thing I was taught to do was volunteer, volunteer, volunteer! Even if you don't know how to do the task, still volunteer, and FIND OUT what you need to do. I would think, *"That's completely overrated. Who signs up for a job they don't know how to do?"* I assumed it built confidence and dedication in a person. I was no stranger to hard work, especially after working at Northrop Grumman Corporation for over twenty years. In that role, I was always willing to take on challenging tasks and learn new responsibilities, which is how I gained confidence and experienced growth in my new leadership role as a campaign manager.

Politics didn't have a place in my future. I was never interested in it, especially when I was in college. So, who would have thought that I would end up working in this field as an administrator for a local politician who sought to run for city council in Hampton, VA in 2012? I then went on to be an administrator for a former Councilman during a re-election campaign in 2014. After two election cycles, I thought I had done pretty well as an administrator, one of my God-given gifts. In 2016, the new Councilwoman asked me to become her campaign manager for her re-election campaign. I was up to the challenge even though I was paralyzed with fear. I had always liked working behind the scenes, being told what to do or what is needed. I researched online and even purchased a book on winning local elections. However, I was failing miserably at the job by not delegating tasks and taking on too much work for myself. I was not being effective and not using the resources and talents of the team. Most of the people on the team were older than me and that plagued me as well. They were more experienced. I was crippled with fear and the campaign suffered because of it.

Imagine yourself in the middle of the ocean DROWNING; that's how I felt as the campaign manager at that time. The Councilwoman noticed I wasn't performing well and gave me a very stern lecture. She called me while at the nail shop and I began to cry in front of everyone. I just SHUT DOWN. I told her I didn't want to do this anymore. I then called another team member and she agreed to take over as campaign manager. I became the deputy campaign manager. I felt like a failure and that I let myself down miserably. Thankfully, however, the re-election ended in victory.

I then retreated to my community service, living my life, and not EVER wanting to go into campaign management again. Great plan, right? WRONG!!! God had another plan. In June 2017, I received a call from a friend asking me to contact her. She wanted to know if I would be interested in being the campaign manager for a local attorney's re-election. I said to myself, *"Oh no, not me,"* and I asked her how my name was mentioned. She said the attorney asked me to assist him in this endeavor. After the paralyzing experience I had before, I was not going to be anybody's campaign manager. The attorney is a Godly man and he could sense my uneasiness about being asked to perform this task; therefore, in his true fashion, he asked me to pray about it. He did let me know he prayed about who to ask to be his campaign manager and I came in his spirit. I prayed about it and inquired with *"seasoned"* people I highly respect and they told me to go for it. I felt a peace with the decision and once again I was scared to death! However, THIS time I took God as my partner and we did this together.

BEHIND THE SCENES

This experience was different than when I was the Councilwoman's campaign manager in 2016 because the attorney trusted me and gave me complete control over the campaign. Managing campaigns is NOT easy and I stayed on my knees in prayer. Positive that I was making the right decisions, I used my resources to assist me in this task. One thing I was always afraid of was FAILURE. I am my biggest critic and extremely hard on myself when it comes to a task I am required to do. Well, this campaign ended in a November victory with over sixty-nine percent of the vote in his re-election. Thank you, Lord!! At his victory celebration, I was very teary-eyed because this was the FIRST campaign I had managed on my own. I pushed myself through the feelings of inadequacy, low confidence, and fear and came out on the other side. This is when the confidence within myself shifted and I said, *"Ok Lord, I CAN do this!"*

I had only one month to rest for the holidays because in January 2018, another Councilman asked me to manage his campaign re-election with the election day occurring in May. Again, I prayed about it and said YES!! All God wants is a YES to accomplish within you what He wants to do through you. When you are working with candidates, you remember that they all have different leadership styles and you have to adhere to them and act accordingly. The Councilman was heavily involved in all the details of his campaign, wanting to know all the details of who, what, when, how, and why. He made me a better campaign manager because he challenged me with questions and he needed to have the right answers. I appreciate the Councilman a lot because he taught me to "never give anyone a stick to hit you over the head with." In other words, make sure your "I's" are dotted, your "T's" are crossed, and you always do the right thing. The Councilman's campaign ended in a May victory. My confidence level soared at this point and I thanked God for it. Surprisingly, I realized I liked managing campaigns, so I took on another one, not knowing the complicated twists and turns this next re-election campaign would bring.

In January 2020 the Councilwoman was up for re-election again. Now this campaign was really different and had my head racing because I had to switch gears in the middle of the campaign due to the pandemic. Talk about fear! We had a great team and were creative with our campaign tasks and ways to tell the voters about her to garner as much support as possible. I am very proud to say this race ended in victory. Overall, these elected officials pushed me to do my best. It was necessary and it made me better. In June 2021, that same Councilwoman was elected the Democratic nominee for Treasurer in our city. With no opposition for the election in November 2021, she will become the first African American Treasurer in Hampton, VA.

Belief was my vehicle to conquer my fear. Once I believed I could, then I did. I accepted feedback and constructive criticism from my mentors and advisors. After the 2016 campaign, I began to fully think and work as a leader for future campaigns. I communed with God on every decision and challenge and used Bible verse 2 Timothy 1:7 as my guide. The campaign staff were used in their areas of expertise and strengths, and I began to look at any challenges as opportunities to learn and grow.

You have to understand that your past failures are going to influence your future success. Learn from the failure, note the mistakes, recalibrate and move forward to the next God-given assignment. You will begin to build confidence and trust yourself. I began to use my resources and embrace the role of the campaign manager. I took my work seriously, held the staff accountable for their roles and duties on the campaign, and took the candidate's spirit and vision and made it my own. I became enthusiastic about the opportunities and embraced the challenges. Leaders show up in various forms and I am glad I was able to work with different styles of leaders to learn and help me grow. You do a lot of work in six to nine months for ONE day: Election Day! I have learned in anything you do it will not be easy; do it anyway and do it scared! Accept the changes and ask for help when needed. Always look at the positive and keep your head to the sky because HE is nigh!! Throughout my journey I learned that the one thing I have always had, which I didn't know I had in the beginning, is COURAGE!

Reflections

....

....

....

....

....

....

....

....

....

....

....

....

....

....

....

....

....

....

....

....

....

....

....

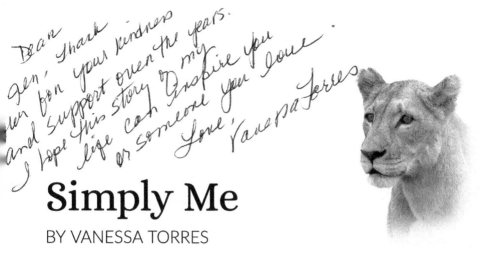

Dear
Gen, Thank
you for your kindness
and support over the years.
I hope this story of my
life can inspire you
or someone you love.
Love, Vanessa Torres

Simply Me

BY VANESSA TORRES

A FEW YEARS AGO, I volunteered to be a presenter at a women's conference. I was excited to finally tell my testimony after years of suppressing my true identity as a bold woman of God! When asked for a bio, I decided to rewrite a new and fresh memoir. I did not want anyone to know where I worked or even have preconceived ideas about me or my career path. As I began to write my bio, it began like this: Vanessa Torres is…

I got writer's block. I simply was. I realized that without my seemingly admirable work experience, degrees, and awards, I was nothing. I was just Vanessa. For most of my life I was defined by my qualifications as a leader. To others, I appeared ambitious, but only I knew that my lifelong desire to achieve success and notoriety was propelled by low self-esteem, lack of confidence, and an overarching fear. This is where my story begins…

Even before I knew its definition, fear defined me. She lied to me and kept me living in despair, debilitating me for decades. I was afraid to be a nobody, so she kept me on a constant search for power, wealth, and validation. I longed to be a good wife and nurturing mother, but fear said I was worthless. At ten years old, I was scared and embarrassed to tell my mother what her husband was doing to me. I was confused and guilt-ridden over his sexual abuse and the things he would make me watch. I felt humiliated, violated — uncomfortable. I was no longer innocent; I was dirty — that's what fear said.

79

At random moments, while playing with my friends, fear would rear her ugly head and say, *"Stop laughing, you are not normal."* She forced me to remember what was happening to me behind closed doors. I kept my abuse a secret to protect my loved ones from sadness. My mother had just given birth to my brother and everyone at home was happy. We went to church regularly and our family was well-liked. Why would I ruin that? Each time I summoned the inner strength to tell, fear made an appearance and said, *"You cannot tell everything,"* so I clammed up.

As I remained silent, the abuse progressed, but one day, I mustered up the courage to provide a snippet of my indignity to my mother. Just as fear warned me, my family was turned upside down. My mother did the right thing and involved authorities, but that was the day fear made her home in my mind. Subsequently, my family was torn apart. My infant brother, my five-year old sister, my mother, and I, were placed under the care of Child Protective Services. For what seemed like months, we lived in foster homes. In the beginning we were together, but later I was separated from everyone and placed in a girls' home. To this day, I do not know the details surrounding this decision. I was too young to comprehend the care-taking role of the system and I have decided not to put my mother through unnecessary pain by asking questions and causing her to reminisce. I missed my siblings, I needed my mommy, and I longed for my friends. Fear said, *"That's what you get for telling."* Although I was too young to recognize the legal process I was undergoing, I was confident that I was responsible for the heartache my mother was enduring. I learned to suppress my deep-rooted anguish. There was only anger, sadness… and my lifelong partner, fear, telling me I was discarded.

With no comfort and no one to talk to about my life, I began making unhealthy choices as a teenager. I experimented with boys and engaged in promiscuous behaviors. Fear brought dissociation, shame, and poor self-esteem into my life; being promiscuous became a common experience. I had mastered the mental process of disconnecting from my rational thoughts, feelings, scriptures I knew, and my true sense of identity. Fear told me I could not control my cycle of compulsive behavior and refrain from sexual stimuli. I was too broken to believe otherwise. They say things happen for a reason, and I believe that statement today, but I could not understand how anything I was enduring as a child was in any way positive. I do, however, recall a shift in my thinking around middle school. I suddenly had an elevated sense of empathy for people. What was most interesting was that I could recognize and hand-pick other girls who had gone through similar things. I discerned their behaviors and the way they carried themselves. I felt their emotions, their confusion, and I sensed their secrets. They were the predicted losers, the least popular ones, yet I rooted for them.

At nineteen years old, I took fear and my addiction into my marriage. I attempted to live a normal life, but my husband worked long shifts, and I spent countless hours alone in a one-bedroom apartment with no friends, no support system… no hope. The only thing familiar to me was fear as I waged an endless battle against my sexual and pornography addiction.

Throughout my twenty-five-year marriage, I lived in a state of perpetual mental exhaustion. I was highly involved in church activities and worked diligently to raise my children in a Godly home. I earned degrees and held prestigious positions, all the while struggling with my own habits and pain. I was dishonest with my husband and family, and it weighed heavy on my soul. *"No one is proud of you,"* fear would say. At work I was strong and led with compassion. I have always served in positions of public trust and through the years, many women have openly disclosed traumatic experiences to me. My own story has taught me that this is one of the hardest things any person can do, and I have the utmost respect for these women. I have never shared my own journey for concern that it would impede my position or others' views of me. Serving as the sounding board for the hurting, I learned to dismiss my own need for healing.

In 2015, the feeling of powerlessness became too much to bear. My web of lies, secret relationships, and activities, became unmanageable. I knew I had a problem, but instead of taking responsibility for my actions, I deflected and pressed for a divorce. I was faced with the conundrum of trying to find healing and happiness. I exercised, went out with my friends, worked longer hours, and became involved in social clubs to prevent myself from relapsing into compulsive behaviors. Ironically, I found inner peace one Sunday morning. Boredom led me to open my Bible as I drank my coffee and meditated on my life choices. I read through Psalm 23. It was a beautiful reminder of my pre-teen years when I was confident, innocent, and fearless. Immediately, the Lord began talking to me about peace vs. fear. In the presence of peaceful, still waters, God reminded me that fear was the name of the enemy. My anxieties were suddenly extinguished and through hours of repentance, tears, and humility, I kicked fear out of my life once and for all. Everything was not perfect, but what I know for sure is that I was unshackled immediately.

When fear left, courage entered and began cleaning the house. I became involved in a recovery program that addressed my impaired thinking and the root causes of addiction. I learned that my sexual abuse and exposure to pornography as a child altered my way of thinking and behaving. I confronted every heart-wrenching memory with courage by my side. As a result of my experience and therapy, I began working with women who were incarcerated as a way to help them deal with the despair in their lives. It was important for me to share my story with them, and it was a crucial part of my healing process. Despite my role as a leader, I was one of them, except I had been living in a self-made jail with fear as my best friend.

For years, I trained myself to come across as a beacon of confidence, but my inner-self was marred with self-doubt. God healed me and gave me the courage to purge my life of misery and share my struggles with boldness! I have learned that the leadership skills I bring to the table are not wrapped up in college degrees and pay grades. When I strip all of that away, I simply am… the woman of God I am intended to be, and that is enough. My life is a story about crooked paths and bad choices. It is scandalous, yet proper; ugly, yet beautiful; I've been defeated, yet I've succeeded. My story is of courage, strength, and resilience in the face of challenge. I am a lioness, and fear is no longer my master!

Reflections

....

....

....

....

....

....

....

....

....

....

....

....

....

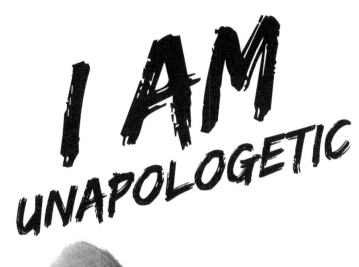

"The unapologetic woman becomes more confident in her skin with each challenge she addresses and every fear she confronts."

Dr. Synetheia

The Lioness Leads Unapologetically

HOW MANY MORE APOLOGIES will we offer for being bold, authentic, and courageous? How many more times will we hide our unique gifts, talents, and abilities so that others feel bigger and stronger? How many more times will we regret speaking up because it made other people uncomfortable? Aren't you tired of apologizing?

Apologizing is the act of feeling or showing regret for some course of action or spoken words. Rendering an apology when we have wronged or hurt someone is the right thing to do. Apologizing for sharing your voice in a room where the majority is saying something different is not correct. Apologizing for being blessed is not right. Apologizing for using the gifts, talents, and abilities given to you by God is not valid. Apologizing to play small or dim our light so that others feel better about themselves is wrong. And yet, so many of us have been trained by people, circumstances, and societal norms to apologize for the wrong things.

The lioness who attacks and devours an antelope does not apologize. By nature, the lioness is a carnivore, which means she lives and is sustained from other meat sources. After a kill, the lioness does not stroll up to a family of antelope and apologize for being a lioness, nor for doing what she must do to survive in the wild. The lioness does not apologize to the buffalo, who can run thirty-five miles per hour like her, but can also easily be caught and taken back to the pride for dinner. She was created to be a lioness and to do what lionesses are designed to do. Why do we apologize for being who we are made to be and fulfilling our divine purpose?

As women who lead, we will apologize for being wrong; this is called taking responsibility and being accountable. Yet when we move as the leaders we've been positioned to be, let's not apologize for doing our jobs. Let's not apologize for our educational accomplishments, expertise, and abilities. Being unapologetic is not being nasty, arrogant, nor unkind to others. It is an attitude and mindset that reflects our confidence, audacity, courage, authenticity, and boldness. The unapologetic woman becomes more confident in her skin with each challenge she addresses and every fear she confronts. Fear works overtime, telling the lie that we will never be accepted if we shine too bright. An unapologetic attitude simply responds, *"I WILL SHINE!"*

We will shine.
We will embrace who we were created to be.
We will not apologize for the greatness and power we possess.

I Am Enough

BY DR.
SHONDA PITTMAN-WINDHAM

SHE WALKED INTO MY OFFICE and angrily yelled, *"Shonda Windham, do not ever give me a directive again! You are not my boss!"* She then turned, walked out, and slammed my door so hard that I was sure it would fall off the hinges. Others came running into the hallway to see what was going on. I sat at my desk in awe for a few minutes before processing what had just happened. I felt three overwhelming emotions within seconds of one another: confusion, embarrassment, and ANGER! I knew immediately that my response was important and could be detrimental to my future, as I was in the middle of an interviewing process to become an administrator. It was imperative for me to respond appropriately because I had far too much to lose.

So, what did I do? I refused to allow my anger to force me to step out of my professional character. I didn't say anything and waited for my supervisor to handle it. When my co-workers came to me furious about the actions of our colleague and shared their opinions of how I should handle the situation, I didn't engage. They gave me all sorts of advice from, *"Go to her space, tell her a piece of your mind…then walk out and slam her door,"* to, *"Slap the taste out of her mouth."* While I must admit that *"Shonda"* was tempted to take some of their creative and humorous advice, I needed to follow the lead of *"Dr. Windham."* Dr. Windham is a bit more poised, proper, and slow to anger. She was trained that way and has developed a disciplined nature that allows her to remain professional at all times. But Shonda? Oh, she is a little feisty and her tongue can be detrimental to one's soul. For this reason, it is rare to see Shonda in a professional setting. I made a choice a long time ago to always take the high road, and I am unapologetic in keeping that promise to myself, no matter the circumstance.

As time went on, I felt judged by my co-workers for not responding the way they had advised me. I was the focus of this colleague's bullying behavior on that day, but many of my co-workers had similar experiences with her, and their responses to the behavior varied. I began to feel embarrassed because I felt like my co-workers took my silence for weakness. They didn't understand that my mind was not on her behavior, it was on my own and how that would impact my future. The most challenging part was not becoming bitter when our leader swept the situation under the rug instead of addressing the unprofessional behavior of my colleague. My leader's failure to hold my colleague accountable was disappointing. I am a strong believer of accountability, and I felt that as a leader, the behavior should have been properly addressed and no longer tolerated among the staff. The respect and admiration I had for her as a leader shifted, and that was tough because she was not only my leader; she was also my friend. I learned to accept that leaders have various leadership styles and that my way wasn't necessarily the right way for everyone.

The very next year, I received my first administrative position and left that particular work site. Within five years, I was promoted three times in my administrative roles. At times, I stand in awe of where I am in life because, statistically, I'm not supposed to be here. Born to a teen mom and raised in a single parent home in one of the poorest areas of Halifax County, North Carolina, some would be surprised at my accomplishments, including me. However, I have always bloomed wherever I was planted despite the highs and lows of life. I am loyal and resilient, and I believe in hard work. I have always held myself to a higher standard without fear of judgment. But over time, I started to question if I deserved to be where I was sitting. I questioned my actions, my decisions, and my abilities because of the road I had to travel to get here. In most professional settings, I am one of few African Americans and at times, the person with the least amount of experience. How could I not question these things about myself? And yet despite my hard work, dedication, and discipline, I still struggle with walking this high, narrow, and sometimes lonely road, unapologetically.

One day, after feeling tired and defeated, my immediate supervisor at the time shared two words with me that I had never heard grouped together before, *"impostor syndrome."* Impostor syndrome is also known as impostor phenomenon and it describes a psychological pattern in which a person doubts their skills and accomplishments despite evidence of their competence. Those two words put everything back into perspective for me. I cannot count the number of days I have felt unworthy of my blessings or accomplishments. But I work hard! I put in long hours, dot my I's and cross my T's, utilize every moment of my day to accomplish tasks, and lead and walk with full integrity and high standard. It is important to me to lead this way and it has proven successful in all areas of my life. I have to believe that who I am and all that I possess is always enough to lead unapologetically. I still have my share of defeated days, but the difference is that now I recognize that I am sitting exactly where God placed me, so I should never apologize for being who He created me to be.

I make a conscious effort daily to walk in my truth. On the days when I don't get it right, I try again with greater intention the next day. My personality and high standards may not win over the masses, but I know that it is what is best and what works for me. I release impostor syndrome daily and I say to myself, **I AM ENOUGH!** To help me maintain, the following action steps guide and help me to live and lead unapologetically every day. Take these steps and make them your own as you continue to stand as an unapologetic leader.

1. **Set healthy boundaries.** Learning to do this changed my life. I learned to make decisions that maintained my accountability, responsibility, and integrity, both personally and professionally.

2. **Just because it needs to be said, doesn't mean that I have to say it.** (God knows I am still working on this one daily!) This supersedes the old saying that it is not what you say, it's how you say it. Sometimes it's just not your message to render. I am slow to share my opinion, but if I am asked, please know that I am unapologetic in my truthful response in my role as both Dr. Windham and Shonda.

3. **Prioritize.** Let go of your search for balance. It doesn't exist. I do the things that are necessary at the given moment. Prioritize and place your focus on what is most important at that time. Thank you, Dr. Synetheia.

4. **Be present.** While working on my doctorate, I would take my laptop EVERYWHERE! I wanted to utilize every free moment I had to work on my dissertation. One day after my youngest son's baseball game, he came running to me to tell me that he made a double play during the game. As we jumped up and down in celebration, I told him that I saw him make the play. He stopped jumping, looked at me in awe and said, *"You did, Mommy?"* After answering him, *"Yes, I was sitting right here watching"*, he said, *"Oh, I thought you were doing your homework like you normally do."* My heart stopped. I cried later that night and I still do when I tell this story. I never took that laptop with me to another event involving my sons. I wanted to be sure that they always knew that I was not just there, but I was PRESENT.

5. **Fill your cup.** A mentor once told me that you cannot pour from an empty cup. Schedule the weekly hair appointment, the monthly massage, the family vacations, the girls' trips. Buy a new outfit. Spend time with God daily. Binge watch on Netflix. Blast your favorite song in the car and sing it like no one can hear you. Most importantly, know that there is no shame in filling your own cup.

6. **Be YOU.** If any part of you makes you uncomfortable, change it. Otherwise, embrace who God created you to be - the good, bad and the ugly - and never apologize for being YOU. This is your life. Live it unapologetically!

Reflections

....

....

....

....

....

....

....

....

....

....

....

....

....

....

....

....

....

....

....

Apologize for What?

BY SHELLI GILLIS

HOW MANY TIMES have you heard the statement, *"Apologize for what?"* Typically, when we hear this statement, someone's words or actions have caused an offense and the offended is seeking an apology. The number of times I have made this statement is countless. As a leader, at some point you may offend a direct report, your manager, or even a peer. I learned this early on when I began my leadership role in corporate America. People are called upon to lead without knowing what leadership is about, what it looks like, and how to do it. Sometimes, people feel that leaders are born with the ability to lead, or those in a leadership role have been equipped with the right tools to lead. I do believe some people are natural leaders, but others may require additional training to be successful. Receiving very little training at the time, I found myself apologizing often for one thing or another. I was a people pleaser and wanted to make everyone happy, and I wondered if my apologies would be viewed as a weakness or undermine my ability to lead successfully. I would soon find out.

In my role as a training coach, I was tasked to assist with the implementation of a new call center site in another state. This required me to demonstrate my leadership skills in unchartered territory. I thought, *"What if I fail? What if I don't adequately train those at the site? What if THEY DON'T ACCEPT ME? What if they don't like me!"* I struggled with these thoughts a lot in the early part of my career. I knew I could do it, but I wanted them to validate my work and approve me as their leader. I would often reflect on some advice I was given to help me in my struggle: *"Being both a people pleaser and a leader would be detrimental to my career and growth."* My task at hand was to manage the team's daily performance, and coach and develop leaders to ensure they would be ready to manage the anticipated call volume.

Upon my arrival to the site, I was asked: *"Are you here for your Dispute by Phone Training?"* *"No, I am here to train your Dispute by Phone managers and representatives."* For a minute, no one said a word. Then there was the two-word response, *"Oh, ok."* I was directed, not escorted, to a room where I would store my work items and computer. Once I placed my items in the training room, I waited for someone to introduce themselves to me, give me a tour of the building, and introduce me to the managers that I would be training along with their teams; but that did not happen.

Prior to the start of training, I also had to meet with the site leader and directors to review my training plan for the week. The leaders onsite barely interacted with me and said I was not adequate enough to complete this assignment. I listened to everyone's concerns and from there I set the tone. As a leader two things will happen in that type of environment: (1) You will become conducive to the environment, or (2) You will shift the atmosphere of the environment. I chose to shift the atmosphere. Why would I not walk in the gift that God had placed in me just to make someone else feel comfortable? I had come with a purpose and mission to accomplish, and that message had to be communicated and executed no matter how others felt about my ability to achieve the goal. I did not spend a lot of time running down my credentials. Instead, I focused on how I would execute my training plan for the week.

In my next meetings with the team managers, their immediate staff and direct reports, I encountered the same response. Questions ranged from *"What made you qualified to come to our site and train us?"* to *"How many years have you been in this leadership role with your company?"* Instead of providing a response that would have shaken the room, my response was simply this: *"My years with the company, my experience with the company, and my results with the company speak to my qualifications."* My response to the direct reports was vague as I did not want to make anyone feel insecure as a leader with the skill set that I brought to the role. However, I then had to ask myself this question: *Why was I nonverbally apologizing for being a great leader?* I knew I was a good leader that was selected to play an intricate role in the implementation of a new call site. Despite the skepticism of others, I was going to do my job.

Once the foundation was set and expectations were given, it was an amazing week of training. While I had to coach a few associates on their behavior, my week of training was successful. Some people will always challenge your leadership if they feel you are not the right person to lead. As a leader, you must address the concerns, but never take it personally. Business is business, and the message and tasks had to be delivered and executed with excellence. If I allowed the criticism of others to impact my ability to lead the charge successfully, I'd always be starting over. I had to get comfortable with knowing that what I had to offer was exactly what the site needed. As a result of my leadership, the site began taking their calls successfully, positive relationships were established, and when I returned to my site, I served as their single point of contact. My time there was definitely a huge success as everyone was able to witness my purpose in spending time with them. I increased my effectiveness as a leader by training new leaders who were just as effective.

Upon my return, my role with the company grew and this growth came with many challenges that I was not ready for. My roles were performance based which meant I was a very disciplined manager when it came to my team's performance. This discipline came with many challenges, disappointments, and oftentimes hurt, but also came with success for many of my associates by way of promotion. Some employees did not want to come to my team, and my response was, *"I know,"* because the bar was set high. To change the perception many had about me, I had to ask myself how I could keep a positive rapport and approach as an unapologetic leader, while still focusing on growth. I did not want my former struggles of people pleasing to resurface. I communicated my long-term goals to my team and consistently discussed career paths. I also enrolled in leadership courses which increased my skills and mindset in how I work with and support my team. I am still a disciplined leader; just a better one.

As Godly leaders who strive to lead with an unapologetic attitude and mindset, we must always remember a few points:

1. We must know our Godly self-worth to understand who we are in Christ, which allows us to walk out what we are called to do.
2. We must cultivate the gifts God has given us, and in turn cultivate the gifts in others that they may not see in themselves.
3. We must be teachable.
4. We must never take *"it"* personally.
5. We must recognize that we lead best when we are passionate about what we are doing.

As an unapologetic leader, you have to cast a vision of long-term growth and success to your staff. You have to help them understand the goals and work that is required and support them in each step along the way. You have to nurture and cultivate the gifts in others and build strong teams to yield high performance. You also have to make difficult decisions and lead with confidence, courage, and passion, knowing that no matter the challenges, the mission must be completed.

An unapologetic leader may never see or hear about the success that has taken place in the lives of those they have managed, but what we know is that when we lead from the heart, it can and will produce good fruit. I received the following message a few months ago that blessed me:

> *"...I wanted to tell you how much I appreciate everything you've done...You dealt with me being hard headed in my early years... To this day, I still use things you've instilled in me as well as a resume you assisted me with. To have had you believe in me and have you as my manager was truly a blessing. Thank you so much!"*

When I stopped worrying about pleasing others, I was able to lead my teams to success, unapologetically.

Reflections

....

....

....

....

....

....

When Fear Whispers

BY MEOSHIA WILSON

DID HE REALLY just ban me from putting my size 9.5 feet in any of his buildings? Wake me up because I must be having a horrible dream! Girl, let me tell you what happened. My mission as a military chaplain was to minister to Airmen's souls and advise commanders on all things religious, spiritual, moral, ethical, and pertaining to unit morale. I knew how to do my job, but I must admit that there were fear whispers I had to combat throughout that deployment. You might identify with some of the fear whispers I experienced: *This is my first deployment; Will my ministry make a difference in people's lives?* The last thing I wanted was to rob God of glory, be ineffective, or be a disruption to the military operation underway. However, one commander accused me of just that: being in the way and distracting his Airmen from their mission. He was used to chaplains only showing up when there was a death in the unit, and even then, he would summon the chaplain. I was in the buildings three times each week, uninvited, to encourage his personnel and inquire about anything unsettling, both personally and professionally. That was part one of my job.

Part two was for me to advise the commander on the trends I observed because low morale impacts a soldier's ability to focus on the mission, do the right things, and do things right. *Fear whisper: What if the commander does not respond well to my advice?* As I contemplated an adverse reaction, I grew uncomfortable because I knew I could help him become a more empathetic and emotionally intelligent leader. Yet, I was unsure if he would trust that my motives were pure. The other piece of this dilemma was that I wanted him to continue accepting me. It was important to me that I fulfill my commitment to part two of my mission: to advise.

I asked God to give me the words to say, and I walked into the commander's office to advise him. Initially, he seemed receptive yet taken aback. He said he would speak with his senior enlisted advisor about the trends I shared. I thanked him for being receptive, and I walked out. Inside I was like, *THANK YOU, JESUS.* A weight was off of my shoulders, and I was hopeful that the commander would improve the conditions that made life in that unit disturbing.

Two weeks later, the commander requested a meeting with me. I thought he wanted to share his action plan with me; not so much. He told me that I was a disruption in his unit. I was trying to undermine his authority. I was no longer permitted to enter any of his buildings. And he said I had been targeting him in my sermons lately. I was devastated and wanted to say the following, with one hand on my hip and the other hand's index finger poking his chest: *Uh excuse me, I'm the only spiritual and mental advocate on this installation. I care about your Airmen, do you? I don't care what kind of chaplain you're used to; I am who God created me to be, and I will rebel against any box you try to put me in. I preach what the Spirit leads me to preach. And as an old seminary professor used to say, if I step on your toes, they must have been in the way!* B-r-e-a-t-h-e, Meesh! Of course, I did not say any of that, but Lord knows I wanted to and would have felt justified, along with being reprimanded, had I done so.

Nevertheless, I told him that his observations were not my intent and I would obey his directive not to enter his buildings. I left with my mind and heart racing. I went to my trailer and hit my knees. I cried. I called my husband and cried some more as I told him what happened.

I cried out to God and expressed how I felt rejected as a person, misunderstood as a pastoral caregiver, and under-valued as an advisor. I was at a crossroad. I could be swallowed up by rejection and fear if I turned left, or I could turn right, dry my tears, hold my head up, adjust my cross and crown, and trust God to walk me through this process. I not only needed His comfort, but His wisdom, as he showed me the lessons I needed to learn, and inspired me to develop the strategy that would help me complete my mission.

As leaders, it would be nice to encounter a heart-wrenching experience and go into hiding while we process what happened, submit to therapy, and heal. But the truth is that we have to develop the stamina and discipline to continue showing up and speaking up unapologetically, without neglecting a deliberate therapeutic process.

So, let me share what I learned as a leader. Self-awareness can help you identify what's normal for you and test the assumptions you're inclined to make about how your norm will or will not be received. When you are on a divine assignment, those who reject you are really rejecting God. Let that go. It's about knowing how to package what you need to deliver based on what you have learned about the recipient. We can learn by observing, but quality advice is best when conversations have already occurred to align your skills with how your boss might like to leverage your skills, if at all. In this story, I failed to have that up-front conversation, and it showed. The conversation may not have prevented him from sanctioning me, but it would have given me better knowledge and understanding of him. God would have given me a wise strategy to advocate for the Airmen, while respecting how the commander wanted to leverage my skills, when summoned.

The other leadership lesson I learned revolves around loyalty. In a hierarchical system, don't be surprised when your boss's boss has his or her back. There is built-in loyalty between them. I did not consider this when I approached the next highest commander to articulate my version of what happened. I expected him to defend me and override the subordinate commander's directive. I was wrong. He supported the subordinate commander and told me to give it some time. That was not what I wanted to hear, but it reminded me that sometimes you have to stand alone for what is right and watch God fight for you. Unbeknownst to me, the Airmen in the unit took the initiative to speak to the superior commander about the subordinate commander's behavior, and they defended me as their advocate. This was evidence of God fighting for me. Meanwhile, I stood still because that's what unapologetic leaders do. Two months later, the superior commander overrode the ban, which restored my access to the Airmen in their buildings.

The final leadership lesson worth sharing is the importance of closing the say-do gap. The say-do gap means your actions should match what your mouth says. Otherwise, there is a gap between the two. I value character, and one of the expressions of character is practicing what I preach. So, my sermons, Bible studies, and inspirational initiatives were designed to refine character so God can transform lives. I felt the need to model what I said by standing tall, remaining respectful, continuing my mission, and maintaining my witness as a follower of Christ. This was vital to me because a say-do gap impacts credibility which erodes trust. If you cannot be trusted, your relationships will suffer, and there goes your chance to contribute to people's lives in a meaningful way and bring God glory.

The next time you find yourself in a situation where someone attempts to silence or sanction you, I encourage you to do the following:

1. Decide in advance to honor God, not your flesh, with whatever will come out of your mouth.
2. Resolve to render, respect and excuse yourself gracefully.
3. Have your moment and allow God to soothe and affirm you.
4. Call a trustworthy person or people who will give you godly counsel and a strategy for moving forward with your mission as you heal.

When fear whispers, you ROAR back! Tell fear that the God who masterfully made you and has you on a specific assignment is with you. He is for you. He will fight for you. He will ensure the weapons that materialize melt before your eyes. And you will not shrink back or *hold your mule*. Say this with me: I will ARISE, unapologetically, to say and do as God instructs me, even if I have to stand alone! Cling to Isaiah 41:10 to overcome crippling fear. And when fear does not entirely go away, DO IT AFRAID! Just don't abort the mission.

Reflections

....

....

....

....

....

....

....

Epilogue

WOW. JUST WOW!! I wasn't ready. I thought I was, but I wasn't.

At the start of this book, I invited you on a literary journey. I introduced you to fourteen amazing women in leadership. I welcomed you into the BACÚ™ Tribe as a lioness who, like each of them, is becoming increasingly bold, authentic, courageous, and unapologetic. I know each of these women, personally. Our leadership paths have crossed in the workplace, Christian ministry, and college. Did I mention that I know each of them personally? At least I thought I did until I took this literary journey with you. I realized that I've known them personally, but I'd not known each of them intimately. Intimacy in any type of relationship is a closeness and familiarity of a private nature. Intimacy is a space where you realize how much you have in common and how transparent you can be with one another at levels that go beyond what's readily seen in public. After taking this journey with you, I realize I share an unspoken intimacy with each of these lionesses because I found a piece of me and my story interwoven into the fabric of their stories.

I've felt the fear on my job like MaRhonda and had to fight to boldly keep showing up in the face of criticism, lies, and acknowledging my own missteps. I've been the woman in ministry, like Rasheena, who struggled to be me and fought to become comfortable in my own skin and accept who I am. Like Nicole, I've been paralyzed by fear of rejection and self-rejection. I've chosen unhealthy coping strategies like overeating then using laxatives to purge so I wouldn't gain weight. Much like Shelli, I've lost track of how many times I've apologized for the authority I possessed while holding a leadership position. Like Charla and Shenay, fear of reprisal or being misunderstood by others kept me silent when I should've spoken up. Like Dr. Shonda, I've had to navigate the minefields in the workplace, and fear lied to me and told me I wasn't enough. Like Leslie, shame and guilt from past decisions have held me captive and silenced me for fear of someone finding out the truth and ferociously judging me. Like Kieshenna and Stephanie, I've struggled with depression and anxiety. Like Courtney, I've doubted my own strength and power yet survived a depth of brokenness that's left me in a fetal position on my bedroom floor. Like Meoshia, I've had to put on my faith in God to overcome personal and professional experiences that wounded me at levels I've never spoken about. Like Vanessa, fear held me captive for so long as I refused to acknowledge my addictive behavior that negatively impacted my relationships. Like Hope, fear has knocked me on my butt, and I had to walk away from everything to regain my confidence and strength.

Can I tell you what happened to me on this journey?

- I shed some tears.
- I did a lot of self-reflection on the role fear has played in my life since childhood and how it still shows up in my life.
- I smiled in amazement as I discovered strengths and resilience in my fellow lionesses that I never knew existed in each of them.
- I applauded and rooted for each of them as I watched them become bolder, more courageous, authentic, and unapologetic about their God-given uniqueness.

So, I'm wondering: where did you find yourself on this journey, and whose stories really hit home for you? Whose story pricked your heart and even left you wiping away a tear or two? How often did you sit back and think about the times fear has overtaken you? Who'd you cheer for? Now, here's the BIG question: How many times did you viciously judge yourself as you compare yourself to some of the stories you read and audibly, or within your heart, said, "I could never be bold, authentic, courageous, or unapologetic like that?"

As I said from the beginning, lioness, there's no coincidence that you have this book in your hand. You needed this book to push you because it's time for you to live and lead boldly, authentically, courageously, and unapologetically.

- You've played small way too long!
- You've shrunk so small so many times that you no longer recognize just how tall you're capable of standing!
- You've compromised your unique mixture of gifts, talents, and abilities so long that most people have no idea just how powerful you really are!
- You've lived under the weight of shame and guilt from the stuff you did years ago that can't be changed. GIRL!! It's time to rise up out of that pit of despair!

I said it before, and I'll say it one more time: fear is a part of all our lives, and none of us can escape its visitation. While we can't avoid it, we can choose to confront it and be bold, authentic, courageous, and unapologetic. You and I can choose to be like the lioness: brave, bold, resilient, courageous, authentic, and unapologetic. We can choose to take these stories we've read and use them as fuel to press us beyond fear. IT'S TIME! You know what fear feels like. Aren't you ready to experience how it feels to be BACÚ™? I know you are. You've become accustomed to talking yourself out of it when fear shows up. We ain't doin' that no more, Lioness!

This book is YOUR launch pad to living beyond fear, and like lionesses, we're going to do this as a tribe! None of us have arrived at a place of perfection in living and leading boldly, authentically, courageously, and unapologetically. I'm still a work in progress, and so are you. We're making progress in small and big ways, just like the lionesses in this book. Let's keep that same energy going by connecting in a space designed just for women in leadership.

Meet me at <u>www.synetheia.com/bacutribe</u> and let's ROARRRR TOGETHER!

MEET
THE AUTHORS

Dr. Synetheia N. Newby

Dr. Synetheia N. Newby is *The Purpose Cultivator*, helping individuals make the environment of their lives conducive for living IN and ON purpose! She is the Owner and Founder of *I Am Dr. Newby Global LLC*, President and Lead Consultant of *Greater Works Global Solutions LLC*, and the creator of the BACÚ™ brand. Dr. Synetheia encourages individuals to live and lead boldly, authentically, courageously, and unapologetically! She also hosts *The Lioness Den*, a podcast for courageous conversations with women who lead.

Dr. Synetheia is an international speaker and national training consultant with over twenty years of demonstrated and dynamic experience as a motivational speaker, training specialist, organizational strategist, and coach. Dr. Synetheia's essential areas of expertise include leadership development, personal development, crisis intervention, and management. She possesses over twenty years of experience as a leadership development trainer, local government executive, executive leader in non-profit and faith-based sectors, and an entrepreneurial leader. As an author, Dr. Synetheia has written three e-books and coauthored a daily devotional entitled *One DAE at a Time: Intentional Declarations, Affirmations, and Encouragement for Women.* Her first published work, *The Liberated Leader: Leading UP from the INSIDE OUT*, is scheduled for release in 2022.

Dr. Synetheia holds a Bachelor of Science degree in Criminal Justice and a Master of Science degree in Human Resources Management with a Human and Organizational Development concentration. She earned a doctorate in Strategic Leadership with a concentration in Leadership Coaching from Regent University.

Contact Info

Author Page: www.purposedpublishingcompany.com/iamdrnewby
Email: snn@iamdrnewby.com
Facebook: www.facebook.com/iamdrnewby
Instagram: www.instagram.com/iamdrnewby
LinkedIn: www.linkedin.com/in/iamdrnewby
Twitter: www.twitter.com/iamdrnewby
Website: www.synetheia.com

MaRhonda Echols

MaRhonda Echols was born and raised in Danville, Virginia, and currently resides in the Hampton Roads area of Virginia. Upon completion of her B.S. Degree in Human Services from Old Dominion University, she began her career in the Criminal Justice and Human Services field. She has worked as a Victim's Advocate in the local prosecutor's office to serve youth and families that have been victims of a crime and are now involved in the criminal justice system. She has also been a community outreach coordinator, and a program manager for an initiative focused on providing positive opportunities to youth and young adults that have identified as gang members or at-risk youth. In that position, she also helped to start a summer work program that was responsible for providing work training and experiences to over 1500 youth and young adults over a five-year period. She currently serves as a community resource coordinator in which she is responsible for connecting youth and families to needed services in partnership with the local law enforcement agency.

In addition to her professional career, MaRhonda is very active in her local church, Christ Church Ministry in Hampton, VA. She has served in various capacities, such as president and advisor to the Young People's Auxiliary, Christian Education facilitator, choir director, media ministry, and other capacities as needed. She is passionate about serving young people and grateful that she has been allowed to do so in both her professional and church life.

Contact Info

Author Page: www.purposedpublishing.com/mechols
Email: marhondae@gmail.com
Instagram: www.instagram.com/MaRhondae

Stephanie Lane

Stephanie Lane resides in Lubbock, Texas. She is the mother of her twenty-five-year-old son and eight-year-old daughter, who are her world. Stephanie is an entrepreneur and owns multiple businesses, including Unique Butterfly Blings and Uniquely Thirty-One. She currently works with individuals with intellectual disabilities and has worked in this field for over fourteen years. Stephanie is currently pursuing a bachelor's degree in Criminal Justice, and her hobbies include reading and shopping online.

Contact Info

Author Page: www.purposedpublishingcompany.com/slane
Email: stephanielb7@aol.com
Instagram: www.instagram.com/kailove03
Facebook: www.facebook.com/profile.php?id=100004818942488

Leslie Billups

Minister Leslie Billups has been involved in the dance ministry for nineteen years, and currently serves as the Team Administrator. She began dancing in July 2000 with Harmonious Voices for Christ Praise Dance Company under the leadership of Co-Pastor Alicia Dudley. Although she became interested in the ministry of Mime in 2008, it was not until 2010 that she began to truly accept the call of ministry that God has placed in her life.

Leslie decided to move on and further her studies of the Worship and Arts Movement by completing several courses through Eagles International Training Institute. Leslie currently serves as a staff member under Eagles International Training Institute as Mime Instructor, TEN Mime Director, TEN Regional and State Leader, as well as Site Leader.

Leslie obtained her Associates of Science Degree in Interdisciplinary Studies from Kaplan University in December 2010, and her Bachelor of Science Degree in Elementary Education & Special Education from

Grand Canyon University in April 2016. Leslie is the proud founder of LB's Locs and Braids. She is also a Senior Consultant for Thirty-One Gifts and is expanding her role in entrepreneurship.

Leslie's favorite scripture is Jeremiah 29:11 "For I know that plans I have for you, saith the Lord, Plans to prosper and not to fail. To give you hope and a future." She believes and continues to have faith that God will give her total healing and all the desires of her heart. Leslie currently resides in Gloucester, Virginia, with her amazing husband of twenty years and has three talented and anointed children.

Contact Info

Author Page: www.purposedpublishingcompany.com/lbillups
Email: dvynanointed@yahoo.com
Facebook: www.facebook.com/leslie.billups

Nicole Ellis, MBA, PMP

Nicole L. Ellis, MBA, PMP, is a Christian, wife, mother, author, director, poet, minister of dance and drama, an entrepreneur, and a business-woman. She has three beautiful and gifted children; two girls and one boy. Nicole is a talented writer and public speaker. She received her Bachelor of Arts degree from George Mason University, a Master of Business Administration (MBA) degree from Hampton University, and a Project Management Professional (PMP) certification from the Project Management Institute (PMI).

She is a certified leadership coach with Crowned Ministries International Leadership Coaching (CMI-LC) led by John Maxwell. Coach Nik E. is the owner of a spiritual and physical wellness coaching company, Fit for A Purpose, LLC. She is the author of *Reflections of the Son and Fit for A Purpose: A Spiritual Journey to Physical Weight Loss*. She is also the President of a 501(c)(3) non-profit organization, Prideful Products, collecting various personal hygiene products for people who are homeless. Coach Nik E. is a 21st century renaissance woman who strives to inspire, motivate, and encourage others to passionately pursue their purpose.

Contact Info

Author Page: www.purposedpublishingcompany.com/nellis
Email: f4apllc@outlook.com
Website: www.iamnike.com

Shenay Lewis-Hairston

Shenay is a licensed minister of the gospel, minister of dance, entrepreneur, facilitator, and co-author of a 365-day devotional entitled *One DAE at a Time: Intentional Declarations, Affirmations, and Encouragement for Women*. She is the owner of She Shed Creations where she brings fun and creativity together to create personalized gifts for every occasion. Shenay attended Virginia Commonwealth University where she studied Psychology and Social Work. Shenay is the co-founder of Establishing Praise and Worship Dance & Mime Ministry. She leads local dance ministries and travels the United States ministering and teaching dance.

Through her indispensable relationship with God, Shenay manifests the power in which she lives, ministers, and teaches. She has a passion for outreach to the homeless and those in need. Shenay has a mission yearly to provide basic necessities (food, clothing, and toiletries) to those who can't afford it. Her hobbies include traveling, scrapbooking, and shopping with her teenage miracle Goddaughter, Tyara.

Shenay is confident to walk into any assignment the Lord presents to her. She is bold enough to be the *"Unicorn"* in this world, knowing the importance of uniquely celebrating, encouraging, and loving others. She strives to allow others to see the light and great works in her. She is living her whole life to hear the Lord say, *"Well Done!"*

Contact Info

Author Page: www.purposedpublishingcompany.com/shairston
Email: ShenaysSheShed@gmail.com
Instagram: www.instagram.com/shenaymoniquel
Facebook: www.facebook.com/shenaylewis
Website: www.sheshedcreation.com

Charla Armstead

As an educator, counselor, and girl-mom, Charla Armstead spent the last two decades impacting the lives of youth and families. She is driven to advocacy by a passion to equip and empower the underprivileged, voiceless and the vulnerable. Charla and her daughter co-wrote *Deja Donut Girl: Facing the Enemy* to encourage kids to be their own superhero with faith, boldness, and courage. She is also a contributing author in *One DAE at a Time: Intentional Declarations, Affirmations, and Encouragement for Women*, a faith building anthology and daily encouragement for women in every season of life.

Most recently, Charla added the title of entrepreneur, launching an online boutique, Aderet Apparel, LLC. Through this venue, she reminds women they are *"crowned in beauty"* by providing signature women's clothing inspired by her love for both faith and fashion.

A life-long learner, Charla holds a Bachelor of Arts degree in Psychology from the College of William & Mary, a Master of Arts in Counseling and Student Affairs from the University of Maryland College Park, and a Master of Divinity degree from Virginia Union University. An ordained minister, Rev. Charla Armstead has a heart for worship and arts and a desire to both proclaim and explain the Word of God, imparting practical spiritual principles that transform the hearts and lives of believers.

Contact Info

Author Page: www.purposedpublishingcompany.com/carmstead
Email: charla_armstead@yahoo.com
Instagram: www.instagram.com/aderetapparel

Rasheena Harris

Rasheena Harris is the wife of Dr. Marcellus Harris III, and mother of two amazing children, Marlinda, eleven, and Marcellus IV, nine. Rasheena received her master's degree in Education in 2005. She is a Qualified Mental Health Professional for children and adults through the Virginia Board of Counseling. Currently, Mrs. Harris serves as the Executive Director at a therapeutic foster care agency where she oversees several programs and staff members. She serves as a director on the board for The Heart of Giving and the Peninsula Agency on Aging, as commissioner for the Newport News Human Rights Committee, and proudly as a member of the Alpha Kappa Alpha Sorority, Inc. since 2006.

Rasheena is a God-fearing, transparent mover and shaker who is committed to touching as many lives as possible through community work and servant leadership. She is also committed to displaying God's power through her own living example, confirming that you can live out your calling no matter where you are from or what you come up against. She loves supporting and empowering individuals to stay the course to fulfill their destiny. Rasheena is also working on her autobiography, which will be released in 2022.

Contact Info

Author Page: www.purposedpublishingcompany.com/rharris
Email: rasheena24@hotmail.com
Instagram: www.instagram.com/ladyempress757
Facebook: www.facebook.com/rasheena.harris.792

Kieshenna Mabry

Kieshenna Mabry is a lover of God and grateful for the new mercies He gives her daily. She is the proud mother of three sons: Jaequan, Jajuan and Antonio, who motivated her to become the woman she is today. Jaequan is now their personal heavenly angel. Kieshenna earned an Associate degree in Human Services and Medical Assisting and has worked in the healthcare industry for the last sixteen years as a Certified Clinical Medical Assistant (CCMA). As an entrepreneur, Kieshenna launched a small business called Something Sweet Events and Treats and she is an Independent Consultant with Paparazzi Accessories.

Kieshenna is the grandmother of four beautiful grandchildren: Karsen, Karter, Aaron, and Kenzie, and enjoys making memories with each of them. She also enjoys music and singing, and is an active member of the music ministry at her church. Kieshenna loves sunflowers and anything yellow, and plans to travel and enjoy God's beautiful creations. She lives by the words of Psalm 46:5, *"God is within me, I will not fall; God will help me at the break of day,"* and strongly believes we have to cherish each and every moment we are given.

Contact Info

Author Page: www.purposedpublishingcompany.com/kmabry
Email: kieshennamabry@ymail.com
Instagram: www.instagram.com/jaemabrymom
Facebook: www.facebook.com/kieshenna.mabry and www.facebook.com/Something-Sweet-Events-and-Treats-1596600750607642

Courtney Griffin

Courtney Griffin is a native of North Carolina, and currently resides in Jacksonville, Florida. She serves as an oncology chaplain and Supervisory Fellow at Baptist Medical Center. Prior to becoming a Chaplain, she honorably served for fourteen years in the United States Air Force. After her military service she employed her leadership skills in the retail market. She earned a Master of Business Administration from Saint Leo University, and a Master of Divinity with a concentration in Chaplaincy from Regent University.

Courtney holds ordination from the Rivers of Life Christian Center in Fayetteville, North Carolina, and ordination and ecclesiastical endorsement from The Evangelical Church Alliance. Throughout the years she has facilitated youth and adult bible study, served in the women's ministry, and mentored future leaders.

Courtney is an amateur artist, like her mother before her. She utilizes art as a healing medium and to develop a deeper connection between the Creator and the created. She cultivated her love of art as a young child while visiting museums, taking art classes in school, and during her travels abroad as a young adult. She shares her gift of art by featuring her original art through an online gallery, commissioning serval paintings for personal collections, and showcasing her art in a North Carolina gallery.

Courtney is dedicated to a life of service; one that fosters hope, spurs creativity, encourages growth, and develops leaders.

Contact Info

Author Page: www.purposedpublishingcompany.com/cgriffin
Email: courtneyngriffin@yahoo.com
Instagram: www.instagram.com/gyrl22
LinkedIn: www.linkedin.com/in/courtney-griffin-2206061b7

Hope L. Harper

Hope L. Harper is a native of Hampton, Virginia, where she currently resides. She was educated in the City of Hampton Public School system. She graduated with honors from Kecoughtan High School in June 1991, and she graduated from Virginia State University in 1996 with a Bachelor of Science degree in Information Systems and Decision Sciences. During her adolescent years, Hope participated in the Job Training Partnership Act (JTPA) program. She held various youth positions in the Hampton City Council and City Manager's Office from the ages of sixteen to twenty-two, where she worked during the summers. In September 1998, she accepted a position as a System Analyst at Northrop Grumman Corporation where she is still currently employed as a Property Control Support Specialist, and has received awards and certificates in recognition of her achievements.

Currently, Hope is a member of Bethel Temple Church in Hampton, VA. Always with a willingness to serve in the community, Hope has volunteered in administrative and campaign management capacities for various elected officials in the City of Hampton. Currently, she serves on the Board of Directors of the Hampton Roads Community Action Program (formerly OHA) and Y.H. Thomas Community Center where she serves as Vice-President. She is a member of Delta Sigma Theta Sorority, Inc. and Chums, Inc.

Hope enjoys helping others, genealogy, visiting historical sites, shopping, and spending time with her family.

Contact Info

Author Page: www.purposedpublishingcompany.com/hharper
Email: hopeharper2004@msn.com
Facebook - www.facebook.com/hope.l.harper/
LinkedIn - www.linkedin.com/in/hope-harper/-5a363052

Vanessa Torres

Vanessa Torres is an experienced public speaker and creative writer. She has a uniquely empowered voice that shines through in her Butterfly Blogs and book titled Unshackled: The Unfinished Journey. Her goals include sharing her spiritual awakening and how her journey has helped her heal from sexual abuse and shame. Driven by a desire to inspire others, she takes pride in providing motivational content for women who long for restoration and a closer walk with their Creator. Vanessa has over a decade of experience working with diverse and underprivileged communities. She holds a B.A. in Communications and an M.Ed. from the University of Maryland Global Campus.

Contact Info

Author Page: www.purposedpublishingcompany.com/vtorres
Email: vbtorres2011@gmail.com
Blog site: www.freedomfortheforgottenblog.wordpress.com
Amazon Author page: www.amazon.com/~/e/B07NC1GYMZ

Dr. Shonda Pittman-Windham

Dr. Shonda Patrice Pittman-Windham was born and raised in the small, rural town of Tillery in Halifax County, North Carolina. She is an only child raised by a phenomenal single mom who is now her best friend and number one cheerleader. Shonda is married to her college love, Renoldo, and they have two amazing sons, Renoldo Jr. and Rian. She is an education administrator by day, but she is also an adjunct instructor, event planner, soccer and baseball mom, student advocate and lover of traveling and family.

Contact Info

Author Page: www.purposedpublishingcompany.com/drwindham
Email: drspwindham@gmail.com
Twitter: www.twitter.com/shondawindham

Shelli Gillis

Shelli Gillis is the wife of Mark Gillis and the daughter of Gail Cosby. She has worked in the Banking Industry for over twenty-five years in positions for Call Center Management, Training and Facilitation, Mortgages, and currently serves as a Branch Manager.

Shelli is a Member of Gethsemane Baptist Church, under the leader of Dr. Dwight Riddick, Sr. and First Lady Vera Riddick where she serves as a Deaconess, an active member of the S.I.S.T.E.R.S. Ministry, and the P&W Praise Dance Ministry. Her favorite scripture is Joshua 1:8-9 (MSG) *"And don't for a minute let this Book of The Revelation be out of mind. Ponder and meditate on it day and night, making sure you practice everything in it. Then you'll get where you're going; then you'll succeed. Haven't I commanded you? Strength! Courage! Don't be timid; don't get discouraged. God, your God, is with you every step you take."*

Contact Info

Author Page: www.purposedpublishingcompany.com/sgillis

Email: scosbymoran@yahoo.com

Instagram: www.instagram.com/shellil1214/

Facebook: www.facebook.com/shelli.gillis.1

Meoshia Wilson

Meoshia counts it a privilege to be a Chaplain in the United States Air Force with nineteen years of service. She is also a Prepare-Enrich Marriage Facilitator and Counselor, a Financial Coach Master Trainer, a LivingWorks safeTALK Suicide Prevention Facilitator, and has 2,000 hours of Clinical Pastoral Education. Meoshia has her Master of Divinity degree, an MA in Marriage and Family Therapy, a Master of Military Studies, and a Bachelor of Science degree in Human Development and Family Sciences. She is currently completing a Doctor of Ministry degree in Military Chaplaincy. She is also a co-author of the devotional book, *One DAE at a Time: Intentional Declarations, Affirmations, and Encouragement for Women.*

Meoshia considers it an honor to be married to Lawrence J. Wilson, who truly loves her the way Christ loves the Church. Her mission is to thrust people into the fullness of who they are in Christ, so they produce accordingly, in perpetuity.

Contact Info

Author Page: www.purposedpublishingcompany.com/mwilson
Email: meoshia.wilson@hotmail.com
Facebook: www.facebook.com/profile.php?id=100019287420754

Made in the USA
Middletown, DE
11 March 2022

62494504R00086